COC

COOL RISK

How to be Happy in a World of Worry

STEVE MARTIN

bookshaker

First Published in Great Britain 2012 by Bookshaker

Cover illustration © iStockphoto.com/retrorocket

Cartoons © Michael Mittag

Cartoon by Michael Mittag

PRAISE

Having started several businesses, which is certainly a risky thing to do, I could relate to the sentiments in this book, but taking risks confronts all of us almost every day. Steve Martin's *Cool Risk* is both easy to read and enjoyable, with lots of interesting anecdotes. There is a thought-provoking message in there too. Some fairly tricky concepts are explained with expert simplicity. A great little book!

– Peter Hingston, author of the bestselling
Greatest Little Business Book, England.

Steve Martin captures the essence of risk in a unique story-telling manner that is funny, enjoyable and easy to read, playing with the reader's discomfort about risk and the contradictions this entails. Weaving together a delightful potpourri of sources, *Cool Risk* gives the reader a necessary and very welcome shake up on how to live. As perceptions of risk are personal, we are invited to come in and share Steve's rich world of personal perceptions. Hard to put down, charming to read and a must to share.

– Professor David Zaruk,
Risk Perception Management, Belgium.

Using examples from his own life, popular culture, medical research, economics, religion and more, Steve explores our emotional reactions and attitudes to happiness and risk. An enjoyable and thought-provoking read. Highly recommended.

– Andrew Newbigging, Senior Vice President, Research and Development, England.

Steve shows a way of rethinking certain aspects of life, which most likely will lead to a happier mind set. *Cool Risk* is well written, with limericks and cartoons to emphasize various points. This is definitely a worthwhile read. If you want to have some fun and gain interesting insights into a different way of looking at things, do not miss this book.

– Dr. Andreas Koop, Senior Project Manager, Germany.

Steve Martin writes in a light hearted and entertaining way about some quite difficult subjects. He leads the reader gently towards an understanding that taking risks is necessary to achieve happiness. His particular take on happiness is original and gives an opportunity to rethink many of the things we take for granted.

– Dr. Havi Carel, Philosopher and Author, England.

My friend sent a draft of his book.
I had promised 'I'll take a quick look'.
What I found there inside
Made me laugh till I cried.
I quivered and trembled and shook.

The content was all about risk.
At first I thought 'So what?' Tsk, tsk!
The insights were deep
And the learning quite steep
But the outcome surprisingly brisk!

By the time I had put the book down,
I had talked of it all over town:
The lessons I'd learned
And the habits I'd burned.
Now I live without even a frown!

– Tim Woolford-Smith, Australia

CONTENTS

PART TWO: GETTING TO COOL

ACKNOWLEDGMENTS

I would like to thank family members, friends and others whose stories have inspired parts of this book. Some are mentioned by name. Those who are anonymous will probably recognize themselves. The book would not have been possible at all without my wife, Judy. In our partnership, it is she who is the real risk taker.

PROLOGUE

The first clue came at my mother's funeral.

We had just come from the cemetery and there we were, all standing around in the church hall, juggling cups of tea and plates of sausage rolls. An aunt asked me about the book I was writing. I told her the book was about risk. People usually react to this information with a glazed expression and rising panic. I was ready for it. But my aunt's response surprised me. She asked me if the book was autobiographical. I tried to preserve a polite exterior but I laughed to myself. How could a popular book on risk be about me? Perhaps it was the stress. Did this seem like a crazy suggestion only because I had just buried my mother? Or was my aunt being a silly old woman?

After years of studying the subject of risk, I was writing a book to tell people where they were going wrong in their perception of risk. I was setting myself up as an expert. But that's where I was going wrong. I was forgetting that all-important truth: experts are human. My aunt was not a silly woman. She was intelligent and perceptive. The book was going to be much more about me than I had been prepared to admit. Although I did not realize it at the time, I gradually came to accept that I was more risk-averse than I thought I was. I was afraid of taking risks. It was not supposed to be like this.

Working on the book led to me giving a talk at the Decision Science Department of Basel University in Switzerland. After the talk, I spoke to a graduate student who had been in the audience. I asked her about the academic staff. I wanted to understand why they had given me such a hard time. She laughed. 'Don't worry about them,' she said. 'You should try going out for a meal with a group of decision scientists. It's terrible! They take so long to decide what to order.' I had discovered that decision scientists are people who have problems with decisions. I felt better. There is nothing wrong with being a risk expert who has a problem with risk. How many crazy psychiatrists are there? That's what attracted them to the subject in the first place.

Death can often seem to be the worst event imaginable. And yet, death can lead to new life in unexpected ways. Rearrange the letters and a 'funeral' can be 'real fun'. I first experienced the death of somebody close when my father-in-law died. I was living in Belgium at the time and had to travel to England for the funeral. At the airport on my way home, I bought a little book called *Being Happy!* by Andrew Matthews. When my wife got home she cried her way through the book. Less than a week later her brother died.

Death helped us to focus on what was important in life. We decided to take some risks. I resigned my job and set myself up as a freelance consultant. And I started writing a book about risk in my spare time. In due course I became a full-time employee again: a project manager with a pharmaceutical company in Switzerland. Ah, here was an industry that ought to know a thing or two about risk! But, no. The industry had great difficulty taking necessary risks and found it all too easy to take risks that should be avoided. In the end, I'd had enough. I left to concentrate on my risk studies.

I wanted to help people to be cool about risk. I studied the subject of risk from many angles: mathematical, psychological, cultural, religious, historical. What I did not realize for a long time was that I had to start with myself. The evolution of this book has been a journey of self-discovery. My aunt was right. It *was* about me. I tried to answer questions about why I think the way I do. And am I so different from other people? The biggest question of all became: how can I use all this stuff I know about risk to make myself, and those around me, happier?

I am now ready to share some of this. I hope it helps.

EXPERT ADVICE?

Go somewhere new and explore.
Don't worry what might be in store.
Take it all in your stride.
You'll be needing a guide
Who has at least been there before.

PART ONE
WARMING TO RISK

CHAPTER ONE

BEING DIFFERENT

So much for "thinking outside of the box"

Cartoon by Michael Mittag

Weird and Wonderful

It is a balmy summer evening. My wife and I are standing on a bridge, watching the trains make their way in and out of Basel's main station below us. It is our wedding anniversary. So you might imagine we're on our way home after a night out, but you would be wrong. This is it. We came out here just to stand on the bridge and watch the trains. What's more, we often do this. If that strikes you as weird, then your thinking would be supported by the statistical evidence: during our many visits to the railway bridge, we have never seen anyone else doing the same thing.

So what's the attraction of standing on a bridge, contemplating the evening traffic at Basel railway station? Let's be clear, my wife and I are not train-spotters, far from it. We know nothing about trains. That's part of the fascination. The whole mysterious ballet is complex and surprising. Powerful engines lurk in the shadows, growling and trembling, before lumbering into action at an unseen signal. Long trains squeal as they jostle for position on perilously tangled tracks. And yet, we are confident that everything will work out as it should – chaos planned with Swiss precision. The whole spectacle creates a sensation of everything being right with the world. All this against a backdrop of the sunset and shared with your dearest companion. What more could you want on your wedding anniversary?

This weird twilight display of chaos and order takes place every night, driven by an invisible power. There are, in fact, several yellow signs on 'our' bridge warning against touching the high-voltage cables. They cry out, '*Lebensgefahr*', which literally means 'life danger'. In much the same way, we talk about 'life insurance' when the insured risk is not life but death. Life always ends in death, of course, but on the way from birth to death wonderful experiences wait to unfold. They can be discovered by taking chances, by doing something a little bit weird.

Although this chapter is called *Being Different* it does not expect you to change – to become somebody different. It is more about understanding and accepting yourself as different from other people. You don't have to find yourself a railway bridge where you can go and watch the sunset. If that works for you, great! However, there's probably some other weird thing you do that helps you to relax, to get life in perspective or strengthen a relationship that's important to you. So go on, do it! (Oh, alright, even if it is fishing.)

WONDERFUL

It wasn't as bad as I feared.
My sadness has quite disappeared.
Not by thinking profound
But the other way round.
I just had to do something weird.

Chance Would Be a Fine Thing

When the Society for Risk Analysis was created in 1980, one of the first tasks they set themselves was to answer the question: what do we mean by risk? They set up a committee. After wrestling with the challenge for four years, they gave up. Defining risk turned out to be too hard. It seems a simple enough question. When you think about it though, it's not easy to define risk. You have to sneak up on it.

Let me tell you a story:

> Once upon a time, deep in the forest in the heart of England, there lived a band of outlaws. Their leader was a man renowned for his skill with the longbow.

3

That's how the story begins. The rest you know because the legend of Robin Hood has been told and retold for hundreds of years in ballads, books, movies and on TV. It's a story about heroism and adventure. It's a story about risk.

This is how many of us prefer to experience risk: second hand, long ago and far away. Risk is like a jacket. It looks great when you see it on somebody else but you wouldn't dream of wearing such a thing yourself. We love to take risks, but we prefer to do it from a safe distance. That's why we enjoy adventure stories like Robin Hood. We can experience the excitement, as the hero plunges into danger, while our real selves sit comfortably out of harm's way.

Risk involves uncertainty. That much is certain. Without uncertainty there can be no risk – and without risk no excitement, no adventure. We sometimes think we would prefer certainty but there is no place for heroes in a world of certainty. Adventure stories, from Robin Hood to Indiana Jones and Luke Skywalker, revolve around heroes who take risks. But there's something else about heroes, apart from the fact they take risks: heroes are goodies.

Heroes don't take risks just for the thrill of it. There's always a good cause. So, where does that leave Robin Hood and his companions? They are outlaws, persecuted by the authorities. They survive by poaching the king's deer and robbing wealthy travellers. Doesn't sound good, exactly. But popular sympathies have always been with the poacher rather than the gamekeeper. Robin Hood famously steals from the rich to help the poor. He fights against unfair distribution of wealth and the abuse of power. He is a goodie after all.

Another thing about risk: it involves some sort of sacrifice. There's a possibility of losing something and this is what makes us afraid of risk. The potential loss could take many forms: loss of money, loss of dignity, loss of status. For a sufficiently worthwhile ideal, a hero is willing to sacrifice everything, even life itself. Fortunately, not every risky choice has death as a possible outcome, but every risk worth taking involves some level of heroism.

In short, we can say that risk involves three things: uncertainty, a worthwhile goal and a potential loss. Not quite a definition but enough to be going on with.

HEROISM

In this age of TV and the web
Ideals are at a low ebb.
A hero takes chances
So goodness advances.
If not, then he's just a celeb.

5

What's Normal?

Coming to terms with risk, then, calls for some familiarity with uncertainty and chance. It means we need to distinguish between what's weird and what's normal. These are hot topics of research among psychologists, so don't expect complete answers. I hope to lead you in a dance around the fire, getting just close enough to feel the warm glow without getting burned. The first steps in this dance lead us into the world of randomness.

In 2005, Apple launched the 'iPod shuffle', a portable music player whose main feature was the ability to play a selection of music tracks in a random sequence. The marketing included slogans such as 'Give chance a chance', 'Life is random!' and 'Enjoy uncertainty'. Some people complained – but not because they didn't like the idea of randomness. The reason they complained was because they didn't believe the 'shuffle' was random. How was it that, with over 60 hours of music on the player, they heard the same song three times in one day? Apple insisted it *was* random. Nevertheless, they introduced a new feature in response to the complaints, called 'smart shuffle'. They said, 'We're making it less random to make it feel more random'.

That's how it is with randomness. Mathematicians have come up with various definitions of randomness. However, for most people, randomness is not something defined by mathematics. It is something you 'feel'. Actually, to be fair to the mathematicians, one of their definitions of randomness *does* fit the way ordinary people see things. It is related to complexity. Basically the definition says: 'the more complicated something is, the more random it appears'. We humans are pattern-matching creatures, searching for things that we recognise wherever we look. We can see faces in clouds and even make something out of an ink-blot. If we can't find a pattern, we call it random. In other words, if we can't explain it, then it's random.

Until recently, I thought this was a modern idea: that what we see as random is just something we don't understand. That was until I discovered Democritus. He was an ancient Greek philosopher who lived around 400 BC. He lived and worked in a remote part of Greece, far from Athens. The heavy-duty thinkers in the capital looked down on him. But Democritus was a big thinker himself. He was one of the first to come up with the idea of all matter being made up of atoms.

He also had the idea that our perception of randomness was due to a lack of knowledge. He apparently liked to use the following example. Two men agreed to send their slaves to fetch water at the same time because they wanted the slaves to meet. When the slaves met at the well, they thought it was a coincidence and put it down to randomness.

SBOEPNOFTT

When we say that things happen at random
It doesn't mean nobody planned them.
Although at first glance
They depend upon chance
It just means we can't understand them.

How Weird Is That?

Understanding what's normal is necessary for a cool attitude to risk. It leads to a balanced view of the world and can help you feel good about yourself. Perhaps it's more helpful to think about what's *natural* rather than what's *normal*. In the natural world there is a great diversity. When it comes down to it, every one of us is weird in one way or another. We're all different and that's good.

Take height for example. There are tall people and short people but most are somewhere near the middle. Your height as an adult depends mainly on your genes and your childhood circumstances. There's very little you can do to change it. That's just your luck. If you're one of the few at the top end of the spectrum – a very tall person – then you probably get frustrated trying to buy clothes, you're uncomfortable riding public transport and fed up with being asked, 'What's the weather like up there?' But there are advantages to being tall, and not only for basketball players.

At the other end of the spectrum – a very short person – you face some of the same difficulties as tall people. Shopping for clothes is a challenge and the thoughtless remarks can be annoying. More than that, short people face very real disadvantages: social rejection, employment discrimination and health problems. The reasons for all this are complicated but one of the factors is our inability to accept something different from average as normal.

Physical height is only one of many individual characteristics. Personalities, for example, are also very different. We talk about somebody being an introvert or an extrovert, but it's not that black and white. Personalities vary gradually over a continuous range. At one end of the introvert/extrovert spectrum is the computer geek while at the other extreme is the party freak. Most people are somewhere in between.

Even if you're of average height and have a typical personality, there'll be something that makes you special. Remember, we're all weird in some way. So make the most of what you've got. It's a lot easier than striving to be something you're not cut out for. If you're short, you're not going to make a great basketball player. On the other hand, don't set your sights on being a jockey if you can't stand horses. Play to your own strengths, not other people's. Don't be content with average. Be outstanding in your own exceptional way.

Cartoon by Michael Mittag

Living Life in Colour

In the 1991 film version of *Robin Hood: Prince of Thieves*, Robin has a Moorish companion, Azeem. When Little John's daughter meets Azeem, she asks him about his skin colour.

Girl: Did God paint you?

Azeem: Did God paint me? [*He smiles.*] For certain.

Girl: Why?

Azeem: Because Allah loves wondrous variety.

The 'wondrous variety' in the world is important. Rejoicing in this variety is what I call living life in colour. (I adopted this expression before I discovered that it was used as a recruitment slogan by Her Majesty's Revenue and Customs!) It was Sir Isaac Newton who invented the word 'spectrum'. He used it to describe the range of colours in sunlight. He discovered that he could use a glass prism to separate the colours – the same colours he saw in a rainbow when the sun reappeared after rain. We now use the word 'spectrum' to talk about the range or spread of anything. But the rainbow, with its spectrum of colours, beautifully illustrates the variety of creation.

How many colours are there in a rainbow? When I was at school, we were taught that a rainbow had seven colours: red, orange, yellow, green, blue, indigo, violet. These days, teachers tend to leave indigo out of their rainbow lessons because it's not a colour that children recognise. In fact, indigo never was a common colour name. Newton inserted indigo between blue and violet simply because he wanted to have seven colours in his rainbow. He was a number freak and believed that seven was a magic number. Basically, he made it up! Generations of children have been taught this magical mumbo jumbo in science lessons.

A rainbow does not have seven colours. It has more colours than you could invent names for. If you pick two colours in the rainbow, there is always another one between them that's different, even if only slightly. It's hard to do this experiment with a real rainbow because it's a bit fuzzy, keeps changing, and disappears just when you think you're getting somewhere. But we do know that it is not made up of seven stripes. The colour changes gradually and continuously across the spectrum. We don't try to name all these millions of colours. It would be too complicated.

Living life in colour is to be aware of small differences and to rejoice in them. Variety is the spice of life. We do have to use some simplifications: short and tall, introvert and extrovert, fat and thin, young and old, and so on. But we would do well to remember that these black-and-white descriptions can cloud the colourful variety of life. Life is not black and white. It comes in more than seven varieties.

Social Anxiety Disorder (SAD)

Our modern efficient society,
In trying to deal with anxiety,
Establishes laws
To prevent every cause
But forgets to allow for variety.

Thinking Inside the Box

Asperger's Syndrome is a term used to describe people who have a particular type of difficulty with social interaction, often associated with obsessive thinking and physical clumsiness. The syndrome was first identified in 1944 but it took 50 years to become established as a standard medical diagnosis. It is now widely regarded as a mental disorder that should be diagnosed in childhood and treated by therapy. However, when the condition became well known, mainly through the internet, a funny thing happened. Large numbers of adults looked at the symptoms and said, 'Hey, that's me!' They had never been diagnosed with Asperger's – not even seen a doctor about their condition – but they wanted that label. It explained so much. Some started referring to themselves by the affectionate term, 'Aspies'. After a lifetime of social exclusion and related problems, they found a place to be normal.

A rainbow life full of infinite possibilities may sound attractive in theory, but our human nature finds this idea challenging. In practice, we don't like to be different. We want to be normal. Being colourful seems risky. When we talk about a colourful character, we have in mind someone who is not your average person but somebody a bit special. Just as Newton organized the rainbow into seven stripes, so we sort people into boxes. When we find ourselves outside one box, we look for another one – or create a new box. That's what the Aspies did with the help of their computers. Tall people see themselves as different from normal so they club together to share the joys and frustrations of being tall. Youngsters on the margins of society form gangs, where they feel they can belong.

It feels good to be part of the crowd, to be in the majority. And this warm feeling can help to create the illusion that normal is best. However, this is not the way the world works. Almost by definition, best is not normal. Excellence is extraordinary. This is how we make progress, whether as individuals or as a species. Human beings got where we are today by evolution. That means that some of our ancient ancestors had to be exceptional.

Think of some famous names who have contributed to the development of our modern way of life. Many of them were eccentric or weird. We've already mentioned Newton. He didn't have all the right answers but he was surely one of the founders of modern science. Many of his ideas are still fundamental to science today. Newton was weird. If he were alive today he would likely be joining the Aspies on the internet. Then there's Albert Einstein, a more recent scientific genius, who was well known for his eccentricity. Some researchers believe that both Newton and Einstein match today's diagnostic criteria for Asperger's Syndrome (although of course the diagnosis was not available in their day). Hans Asperger, after whom the syndrome is named, wrote positively about the benefits to the individuals and to society when 'Aspies' find an appropriate niche in life.

THAT'S NORMAL

I thought that my brother was strange,
Outside the acceptable range.
Attempts at reform
Were a piss in a storm.
My opinion was all I could change.

Cooking on Gas

By the time you're grown up, you are… well… grown up. You don't get any taller. That's how it is. Adult height is not affected by anything you do as an adult. Your genetic code had a big say in how tall you are. The rest is down to how life treated you as a child. It's similar with other individual characteristics like intelligence and personality. Intelligence is more difficult to measure than height. Personality is even more complicated. We don't know to what extent these things can be changed as an adult. The evidence suggests that it's not a lot. The ingredients you have to work with are pretty much fixed by the time you're a young adult.

It's a bit like the cookery show on TV where two teams are given some food and have to cook a meal using those ingredients. They don't sit around complaining that they've been given a leek and two lemons. They go ahead and create the best dish they can with what they've got. Likewise, it's no use blaming God, parents or your ex for your problems. Blame doesn't change anything.

So it is with your attitude to risk. Do you love taking risks or try your best to avoid them? Your approach to risk-taking is heavily influenced by your genetic make-up. It's also affected by your upbringing. There is a certain level of risk that you are comfortable with. Faced with greater risk, you tend to back off. However, if the risk is lower than your preferred level, you get bored and seek more risk. The level of risk you feel comfortable with is sometimes called your risk thermostat. When the risk gets too hot, you try to cool it. When the risk is too cool, you want to warm things up a bit.

Everybody is different. We each have our own individual risk thermostat. Nevertheless, it is possible to make some generalizations: we get more cautious as we get older, men seek more risks than women and tall people are greater risk-takers than short people. Your risk thermostat is also affected by your mood. When you're afraid, you are less inclined to take risks. When you are angry, you take more risks. The mood change turns your risk thermostat up or down temporarily but then it settles back to its usual level.

The bottom line is this: there's not much you can change. This may not be what you want to hear. You might even think it sounds depressing. But, when you think about it, this is a wonderful optimistic message. It means life is not that hard. You don't need to spend a lot of energy trying to be perfect. Much better to travel through life discovering your imperfect self and using this discovery to your best advantage. It does, most definitely, require change – but not a change to the ingredients. It means understanding the ingredients and changing the recipe. If you're thinking, 'That's easier said than done,' then you're right. You probably don't know how to cook leeks and you might not want to learn. However, it's a whole lot easier cooking leeks than turning leeks into carrots.

BREAKING OUT

I've discovered the door is unbarred
And there's nobody there standing guard.
No longer confined
By the chains in my mind,
I see that life isn't so hard.

Risk Management

When I talk to people about risk, it's usually not long before they mention risk management. Therefore, I should say a few words about it here. 'Risk management' is one of those bits of business jargon that has leaked out into everyday language. Like most office-speak, the expression is not intended to be clearly understood but rather to say something about the speaker. The message that office-speakers hope to convey is that they are familiar with the subject – that they are members of the club – that they are inside the box. Risk management is nothing special. We all do it every day. We decide whether to take a risk or to avoid it. When a new situation presents itself, we work out what to do about it.

Taking risks is not easy for most of us as individuals. Even more challenging is taking risks while sticking to our values. When working with other people, it's even more difficult. That's why the discipline of risk management is necessary. A formal process, often involving numbers, helps to make decisions about risk when many people are involved. But organizations can make the same mistakes as individuals, such as being excessively afraid of change or losing sight of their values. Good risk management is more about knowing where you are today than planning where to go tomorrow – understanding the ingredients before adapting the recipe.

I don't like the expression 'risk management' for two reasons: one is 'risk' and the other is 'management'.

Risk is used in a negative sense. The concept of risk management concentrates on what could go wrong. However, we never take risks so that we can suffer, whether as individuals or in business. We take risks in order to achieve benefits. So, the risks must always be weighed against the benefits.

Management suggests control. The expression 'risk management' can create the impression that risk is something that can be controlled. But risk is about uncertainty and we usually have two choices: avoid it or cope with it. If we avoid the risk, we also give up the chance of getting the benefits. So, risk management is really more about coping with something than controlling it.

Most of all, the problem with risk management, as practised in most organizations, is that it doesn't work. A great deal of time and effort can be expended, creating an illusion of control when in reality the matter might just as well have been left to chance. Douglas Hubbard writes in his 2009 book, *The Failure of Risk Management*:

> The research is overwhelmingly conclusive – much of what has been done in risk management, when measured objectively, has added no value to the issue of managing risks. It may even have made things worse.

BLUE SKY THINKING

Risk management epistemology,
With all its arcane methodology,
Just what does it say
At the end of the day?
It's nearly as good as astrology.

Surprise!

As a Brit who has lived abroad for many years, I am amused by the mystique attached to 'British humour' in other countries. Many non-Brits, even those who enjoy the likes of *Blackadder* and *Monty Python*, find the British sense of humour inscrutable. I could be talking to a Belgian in all seriousness. But if he's struggling to understand me, he might suddenly smile knowingly and say, 'Ah yes, British humour!'

The mysteries of humour, however, are not confined to the British. Many studies have been done, and books published, on the subject of what makes human beings laugh. The most important element of the mystery is surprise.

Surprise is something that breaks a rule that you have in your head. It's not enough for it to be new. It has to be unexpected. If your brother gives you a present every Christmas, it's no surprise when he arrives at the door with a gift-wrapped box. However, if you receive a present at another time, when you're not expecting it, well that's a surprise. You would call it a nice surprise, the kind of surprise that makes you smile. The unexpected or incongruous twist at the end of a joke is what makes you laugh. Surprise can be enjoyable. Children love it. By contrast, the business risk manager can be heard to say, 'We don't want any surprises.'

Surprise can indeed be either nice or nasty. Whichever way it is, though, it's something unexpected or strange and can be amusing. Yes, that's right. A nasty surprise can also be funny. Imagine being in a car, for example, driving along a country road and suddenly getting stuck in a flock of sheep. This may not seem funny at the time, especially if there is some damage to the car. But later on, when you've recovered from the immediate distress, you can laugh about it. The concepts of 'unexpected' and 'amusing' are so closely linked that we use the same word for them: 'funny'.

THAT'S FUNNY

Deal me a difficult hand.
Don't feed me the boring and bland.
I'm one of those guys
Who just loves a surprise –
As long as it's carefully planned.

Chewing the Cud: Chapter One

- There is no place for heroes in a world of certainty.

- Be prepared to sacrifice something for a worthwhile cause.

- Random just means we can't understand it.

- We are all different and that's good.

- Be outstanding in your own exceptional way.

- Live life in colour: celebrate variety.

- Understand the ingredients and change the recipe.

- Enjoy surprises!

CHAPTER TWO

Happiness

The patient is almost cured. He used to suffer from severe delusions of happiness.

Cartoon by Michael Mittag

Happiness and All That Jazz

A story is told about the great jazz trumpeter and singer, Louis Armstrong. He was at a party where a woman asked him, 'What's this thing called jazz?' to which Satchmo replied, 'If you have to ask, you'll never know.' That's how it is with happiness. The more we pursue it, the more elusive it seems. At best, we are able to recognize that we are happy: 'Ah, this is jazz!' But much of the time we are too preoccupied with other kinds of mood music and find it hard to see the jazz influence.

It's not for want of trying. Happiness has been studied extensively by everyone from ancient philosophers to present-day psychologists. And yet, we still don't really know what happiness is, or exactly how to achieve it. Research is difficult when the subject is so hard to define, but some progress has been made in recent years. Studies with identical twins have confirmed that a large measure of our happiness depends on our genes. At least 50% – possibly as much as 80% – of our potential for happiness is inherited. In that respect, happiness is like height, intelligence and so many other aspects of our make-up: there's a part we just have to accept and a part that we can change.

Despite my lifelong fascination with words, I find it difficult to put names to my feelings. I do get emotional but I'm not sure how to describe my feelings. I can get quite upset if someone asks me specific questions about how I feel. Some years ago, I was discussing emotions with the family and somebody mentioned happiness. Without hesitation, I responded, 'Happiness is not an emotion!' Everybody laughed and I backed down, supposing that I had learned a valuable lesson.

Now I'm back where I started. I don't think happiness is an emotion. At least, if it is, it's not like other emotions. Psychologists today can't agree about whether happiness is an emotion, or a mood, or something else. So I feel happy about having my own feelings on the subject. One of the problems with naming things is that there are just not enough words to go round. The word happiness is used for several states of mind that are essentially different. It's almost as if happiness, rather than being a positive emotion, is an absence of negative ones. Thus, it takes only one negative feeling to spoil the party. We speak about being 'unhappy' but never 'unsad'. Happiness is like a perfect crystal that is all too easily cracked.

Whatever it is, happiness is a state of mind we all want for ourselves and our loved ones. This chapter on happiness is a tiny contribution to the vast amount that has been written on the subject. The difference here is the risk angle. Most people would not talk about risk and happiness in the same breath. But the two things are closely related, and not just because they are both tricky to pin down. We never take a risk in order to suffer. No, we take risks basically for more happiness. It does depend on what sort of risk – and what sort of happiness – we are seeking. But, in essence, risk and happiness go hand in hand.

NOT UNHAPPY

The people of Neverabad
Were all predisposed to be glad.
The slightest good thing
That luck happened to bring
Would instantly make them unsad.

The Spectrum of Happiness

The idea of happiness as a state of perfection is not helpful. In order to be happy, we have to be able to enjoy something imperfect – in this life at least! Otherwise, it is too easy to drift into a 'cracked-crystal' mentality, in which any small irritation can make us 'un-happy'. There is nothing wrong with aspiring to perfect happiness – provided we enjoy plenty of imperfect happiness along the way.

'Happy' and 'Sad' are opposites, but we don't flip between these two states. There is a sliding scale. Our levels of happiness (and sadness) sit somewhere in a spectrum – a range from extreme sadness at one end to perfect happiness at the other. This is illustrated in the chart (Figure 1), which shows how the level of happiness varies across the population.

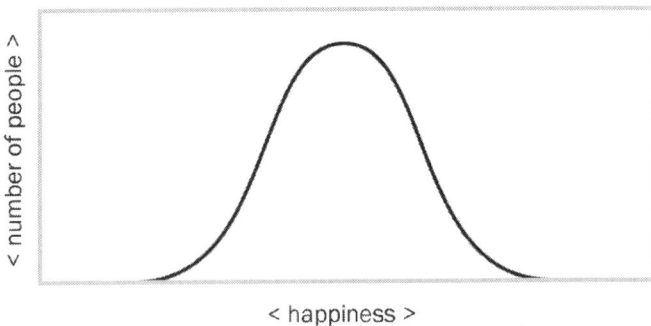

< happiness >

Figure 1

At each side, the curve is low, meaning there are not many people who are extremely unhappy or perfectly happy. In the middle, the curve is high, meaning most people are middling happy.

Table A lists some of the words that can be used to describe a person's happiness. Because these are pairs of opposites, they first seem to reinforce the black-and-white judgement about states of happiness. However, if we look at them more closely, they illustrate the way happiness is a spectrum and not a unique state.

Table A

Sad	Happy
Miserable	Cheerful
Dejected	Elated
Depressed	Flourishing
Gloomy	Bright
Low	High
Blue	Rosy

27

The word pairs at the top of the table describe happiness directly, while those towards the bottom use metaphors like colour, height and so on. Colours are part of a spectrum. When Newton invented the word 'spectrum' it was to describe a range of colours. We now use the word for other things. Human height is a spectrum. A chart showing people's height turns out to be much the same shape as the happiness chart in Figure 1. I am not saying that every tall person is happier than average. That's clearly not true; one grumpy giant disproves the rule. However, studies have shown that, on average, tall people do feel happier than short people.

So, where are you on the happiness spectrum? Of course I don't know, but let's say you are a bit below average. Perhaps your position is like in Figure 2. This might be your position at one moment, but of course it is not always the same. Some days you feel happier than others and your mood can change by the hour. What happens, though, is that your level of happiness tends to return to what psychologists call a 'set point'. This is like the 'risk thermostat' I mentioned earlier and is sometimes called a 'happiness thermostat'.

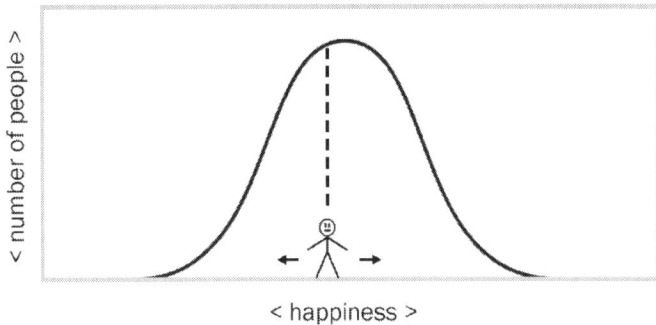

< happiness >

Figure 2

What this means is that your level of happiness can go up and down, as indicated by the arrows in Figure 2, but tends to return to the set point. The set point itself is determined mainly by your genes and early upbringing. The rest is up to you!

THE HAPPINESS SPECTRUM

Between the extremes of perception,
From elation to utter dejection,
Between feeling the blues
And the rosier hues,
There's scope for some blithe imperfection.

Happiness Now

Daniel Gilbert dropped out of school. By the time he was 20, he had a wife, a son and a job. He was struggling to be a science-fiction writer in his spare time. So he decided to enrol at the local community college on a writing course. By the time he got to the college, after a long bus journey, the writing course was full. He decided to go for what was available and signed up for a psychology course. Today, Gilbert is Professor of Psychology at Harvard University and author of the international bestseller *Stumbling on Happiness*.

Gilbert's life story invites us to reflect on the random nature of happiness. His research as a psychologist confirms it. We humans are not good at predicting what will make us happy (or unhappy). That means, generally speaking, we are not good at taking risks. Meet Alfie. He is thinking of buying a car. His thought process goes along these lines: 'Compared to how I feel now, how happy will I be if I have that car?' Alfie is using his imagination to judge how happy he will be in the future behind the wheel of his new car. His imagination might be influenced by ads he has seen, but the decision is based on Alfie's imagination.

So far, so good. Thinking about the future requires imagination. That's not surprising. But Gilbert's research comes to a more surprising conclusion: thinking about the past also uses imagination. We tend to think of memory as a process of recalling facts about the past from where they are stored in our brains. It's not quite like that, though. The brain cannot store and recall all the details we would like. We remember only the key points and the rest has to be filled in by imagination. The recollection may be assisted by a photo or souvenir, but the 'memory' depends to some extent on our imagination, working in the present.

Our feelings about the past, as well as the future, are dominated by our present state of mind. Therefore, as far as happiness is concerned, it is the present that is all-important. How we think about the past depends on how we feel today. The same applies to our thinking about the future. If we can't rely on the past or the future, that only leaves now.

Happiness Now! is the title of a book by Robert Holden, another psychologist, who is director of a business called The Happiness Project. As his book title suggests, Holden stresses the importance of finding happiness *now*, not searching in the past nor relying too much on the future. He also tells us to search inside ourselves for happiness rather than pursuing it elsewhere.

I have to admit that such 'there-is-no-future' talk seemed to me at first a somewhat unattractive view of happiness. This soul-searching, future-proof joy struck me as too restrictive – alright for monks and suchlike, but not for me. I don't want to sit about and meditate; I want to *do* stuff! After some reflection, however, I realized that enjoying happiness now does not mean trying to preserve the present and avoid the future. It does allow for risk and change. Indeed, it *requires* risk and change! Happiness now means enjoying an ever-changing present, progressing from one happy now to the next happy now, surfing the waves of life.

THE TRAIN NOW AT PLATFORM 1

A train pulling into a station
Can offer a good illustration
How the present contrasts
With our futures and pasts –
Where Now is the train, not the station.

All in the Mind

In Uganda, 8% of children die before their first birthday; 31% of the population live in poverty. A friend of mine returned from Uganda where she was doing volunteer work at a children's home in the rural south west of the country. In such remote areas, the statistics are even worse than the national averages. The children at the home are all under two years of age. They are there because their parents have died or cannot cope for one reason or another. My friend has a lot of experience with small children. She says that, despite their difficult circumstances, these Ugandan babies are happy. She shrugs, 'I guess nobody told them they are unhappy.'

Can money buy happiness?

No, my dear, but who needs happiness when you can have Gucci?

Cartoon by Michael Mittag

I have noticed a similar paradox myself during travels in Africa. There are a lot of people – adults as well as children – whose happiness is surprising. They live in conditions that I imagine would make *me* unhappy, but these people are not so. This phenomenon can be seen anywhere in the world, but in Africa there is just so much poverty that the reality is starker. The reality I'm talking about is that happiness does not depend on circumstances as much as we think.

Bad things do happen, of course, but the extent to which they make us unhappy depends on our state of mind – that is, our mental health. An athlete in good physical condition can take some amazing knocks and remain unscathed. A non-athlete subjected to the same knocks would be seriously injured. The reason the athlete is not injured – or is able to recover quickly after injury – is physical fitness. It is similar with mental health. When confronted by a setback, a healthy mind is resilient. First of all, it is not knocked down so low. Secondly, it can recover from the setback more quickly. Happiness is mental fitness.

The happiness spectrum looks almost like the mental health spectrum. Some happiness studies use a scale from 'depressed' at one end to 'flourishing' at the other as a measure of happiness. Happiness is not exactly the same thing as mental health but the two things are closely related. The ability to appreciate 'happiness now' – to seize the moment and realize that you are happy – does depend to a large extent on mental health. A person suffering from depression finds it hard to see anything to be happy about.

SATISFACTION

It is counter-intuitive madness
That poverty lives with such gladness.
But having more stuff –
In excess of enough –
Becomes irresistible sadness.

Happy Endings

The animated film *The Little Mermaid* is based on the fairy tale of the same name by Hans Christian Andersen. The main plot line concerns the mermaid's love for a human prince. The story ends with the mermaid being transformed into a human and marrying the prince. Well, that's how the Disney version ends. The *original* fairy tale ending is nothing like this. In Andersen's version of events, the prince marries somebody else. The mermaid considers murdering the prince on his wedding night but instead throws herself into the sea, where she dissolves into the foam. Andersen later added a slightly happier ending in which the mermaid's soul is raised up as a result of her suffering and loyalty. But this is still a far cry from the Disney happy ending.

The love story in the 2009 sci-fi movie *Avatar* echoes the Disney version of *The Little Mermaid*. The hero, Jake Sully, is paraplegic – a man with useless legs instead of a mermaid with no legs. The bad guy, for his own evil purposes, promises to restore Jake's legs. This is like the deal the sea witch makes with the mermaid. Jake falls in love with a princess of another species; in this case it's an alien race called the Na'vi. The happy ending is the same, albeit with the roles reversed. Jake is released from his human body and becomes a Na'vi warrior, able to claim the princess he loves.

Where does this need a happy ending come from? It hasn't always been like this. While the search for happiness has been going on since ancient times, the expectation that a story should always have a happy ending is a fairly recent development. Some of Shakespeare's most famous plays are tragedies: *Romeo and Juliet*, *Macbeth*, *Hamlet*, *King*

Lear, Othello. No happy endings there. The trend towards happy endings started in the eighteenth century and has been taken to extremes more recently by Hollywood. The happy ending is widely seen as an American invention – so much so that many languages use an English expression for it. In France they speak about *'le happy end'* and in Germany it's *'das Happy End'*.

Daniel Gilbert's research tells us that endings play an important part in our memory of events, both good and bad. It is usually the final part of any sequence that has the most lasting effect on our memory. A film with a happy ending makes us feel good, even if hundreds of innocent people have been slaughtered during the course of the film. The Hollywood marketing machine has known this for years. Shakespeare also knew it. He wrote, in *King Richard II*:

> The setting sun, and music at the close,
> As the last taste of sweets, is sweetest last,
> Writ in remembrance more than things long past.

So, if Shakespeare knew this, why did he write so many plays with unhappy endings? The answer must be that a happy ending was not required to please the audience. It is only in recent times that every fairy tale is expected to have a fairy tale ending.

SHOPPING SPREE

A frenzy of ritual spending
Sustained by an orgy of lending
Climbing the walls
Of the shiniest malls
In search of a happier ending.

The Pursuit of Happiness

The American Declaration of Independence, written in 1776, contains these famous words:

> We hold these truths to be self-evident, that all men are created equal, that they are endowed by their Creator with certain unalienable Rights, that among these are Life, Liberty and the pursuit of Happiness.

There it is – happiness – among the fundamental rights that were considered to be 'self-evident' by the Founding Fathers. But wait a moment. The Founding Fathers were wise. They did not claim that everyone had a right to happiness, only to pursue it. Nor did they attempt to define what they meant by happiness.

There is some uncertainty about what the Founding Fathers themselves understood by the phrase 'the pursuit of Happiness'. Darrin McMahon, in his book *Happiness: A History*, devotes some 20 pages to the matter. One of the things he points out is that 'pursuit' would have been understood in 1776 to mean something different from what it usually means today. Pursuit was a hunt or quest, something that involved a challenge. Pursuit required some sort of struggle. Therefore, 'the pursuit of Happiness' suggests more of an adventure than simply being happily occupied. In a sense, happiness is embodied in the quest rather than being an end in itself.

Many cultures – and perhaps especially that of the United States – tend to forget about the word 'pursuit'. They claim their right to Life, Liberty and Happiness. They see happiness as a goal to be achieved. But worthwhile happiness is not like that. Happiness is more like a way of travelling than a destination. The journey itself is what is to be enjoyed, without any pressure to arrive.

I used to be very bad at long journeys. Even a one-hour train trip would stress me out. I was completely focused on my destination, counting the minutes until the train was due to get there. Over the years, I have learned to enjoy the journey – but only as long as there is no pressure to arrive by a certain time. On my first trip to sub-Saharan Africa, my family and I took a long-distance bus from Johannesburg in South Africa to Bulawayo in Zimbabwe. Soon after breakfast, the bus got a puncture. All the passengers piled out. We were on a tarmac road, but in the middle of nowhere. You might suppose that we were disappointed, annoyed or distressed. Not at all. We were happy. We felt that our African adventure had really begun.

The two drivers took two hours to change the wheel. (You know how difficult it can be to get the wheel nuts off using the gizmo in the toolkit.) The spare did not have enough air in it, so we had to proceed at a reduced speed. Then there were roadworks. The bus left the tarmac and headed off across the dirt, eventually arriving in Bulawayo four hours late. This was in the days before the African mobile phone revolution. I phoned from a shop with a sign that read, 'Please do not ask to use the phone'. When our host arrived to pick us up, she shrugged and said 'This is Africa'. Nobody was unhappy.

LIFE'S JOURNEY
It's wonderful being alive –
To flourish and not just survive.
Yes, life is a quest
That is really the best.
I'm sure I don't want to arrive.

Foolishness and Fun

The BBC series *The Choir: Boys Don't Sing* was reality TV at its best. It won the Best Feature award at the British Academy Television Awards 2009. The series featured choirmaster Gareth Malone as he built a 100-strong choir at an all boys specialist sports college. In the first episode, at school assembly, the

Head Teacher introduced Mr Malone as a new member of the Music Department. The boyish-looking, young teacher smiled at the assembly of teenage testosterone:

> Good morning, gentlemen. I would suspect that a lot of you got to year six quite happily singing and then made the transition to come to year seven and you start to feel a bit embarrassed about singing. I want to say that singing is a perfectly good thing to do for young men. So I thought that I should sing you a song. It's *She's Like the Swallow*. I have to get a note from my recorder…

So he found the note on his recorder and then sang, unaccompanied, a traditional love song – a song that was almost certainly unknown to anyone else in the hall. There was a ripple of embarrassment among the boys. Malone said later, 'It was a deliberate choice not to sing something traditionally manly, to show them that it's OK to sing something sensitive.' Was he brave? Was he foolish? Yes to both. And it worked. Malone's cool courage earned him the respect of many of the boys. Audiences and critics were similarly impressed when they saw it on television. Definitely a cool risk.

Although his assembly singing stunt went well, Malone still had an uphill struggle to pull together his boys choir. The reason many of them rejected the idea of singing was their fear of looking foolish. They were lacking in self-confidence and also unable to appreciate the benefits of being in the choir. They were not prepared to take the risk of signing up because the loss they feared – the respect of their peers – loomed larger than any possible gain.

The fact is, a genuine search for happiness often involves a measure of foolishness. We risk putting ourselves into a situation where we might look or feel foolish. It is not that feeling foolish makes us happy – quite the opposite – but it is often necessary to break through the foolishness barrier in order to find happiness on the other side. Gareth Malone himself said about his TV series: 'I look like an utter twit most of the time.' Nevertheless, I am sure he is happy that he did it. And he made a lot of other people happy too.

Foolishness should not to be confused with fun, although the two words are related. Fun is sometimes used simply as another word for happiness and, in that sense, it is alright. However, fun can also be about making other people look foolish, as in 'making fun of' someone. This kind of fun is clearly not a path to real happiness. Fun tends to involve foolishness without any worthwhile purpose.

FOOLISH ADVICE

Being foolish can have an effect
That people tend not to expect.
To act willy-nilly,
Although it feels silly,
Can actually lead to respect.

The Joy of Risk

Edgar Rombauer suffered from mental illness – or 'nervous attacks' as they were called at the time. One day in 1930, while his wife Irma was out shopping, he shot himself in the head. Irma Rombauer was a strong woman. She realized that she needed an income and set about publishing a cookbook, although she had no experience of writing – nor even any great talent for cooking. The following year she was selling her first book: *The Joy of Cooking*.

The cookbook became an American classic, selling more than 18 million copies over many editions. The New York Public Library chose it as one of the 150 most important and influential books of the 20th century. Its influence was indeed far reaching. When Alex Comfort published *The Joy of Sex* in 1972, he clearly had Rombauer's famous cookbook in mind. In addition to the title itself '*The Joy of...*', the cookery theme is reflected in the subtitle ('A Gourmet Guide to Lovemaking') and chapter headings, such as

'Starters', 'Main Courses' and 'Sauces and Pickles'. *The Joy of Sex* spent eleven weeks at the top of the New York Times bestseller list.

The message contained in both these famous books is that ordinary people can do it and enjoy it. Cooking and sex may be necessary and messy but they can also be fun. And this, I'm afraid, is what 'joy' means to the modern reader of English. When I talk about 'worthwhile happiness', I am trying to put over a sense of happiness with a higher value than fun. Many people say to me, 'Oh, you mean joy!' But I do not want to use that word. If 'joy' has a special place in your heart, by all means use it. But for me the word is simply old fashioned. That's what happens to words; they fall out of use or change their meanings. When Rombauer named her cookbook *The Joy of Cooking*, it was a word of her time. Back then, people could still speak about 'social intercourse' and 'gay musical gatherings'. These days 'gay intercourse' is something quite different!

Christians, in particular, like to speak about joy instead of happiness. They point to the fact that 'happiness' does not appear at all in the *King James Bible* whereas 'joy' makes 155 appearances. They say happiness depends on circumstances whereas joy is more deep-seated. I think it is just word fashion. Let me quote from the Good Book:

Again, the kingdom of heaven is like unto treasure hid in a field; the which when a man hath found, he hideth, and for joy thereof goeth and selleth all that he hath, and buyeth that field. [Matthew 13:44]

First of all the text is old fashioned. We don't use words like 'thereof' and 'goeth' any more so why should we use 'joy'? More importantly, the joy being felt by the man in this passage is the result of happening to find some buried treasure in a field. He is responding to a happy circumstance – exactly what we now call happiness.

When we look at other languages, we see that attempting to make a clear distinction between joy and happiness fails. I tried this with some Brazilian friends and they were unable to make such a distinction in Portuguese. When Germans speak about being happy they usually use *freuen*, which is related to *Freude* (joy). 'Happy birthday' in French is *'joyeux anniversaire'*.

CHEERS!

A drunkard, bereft of employ,
He seeketh the Very McCoy.
He goeth and trieth
All liquor he spieth,
Exulting in transports of joy!

Chewing the Cud: Chapter Two

- Happiness is like a perfect crystal.

- Enjoy imperfect happiness.

- Don't rely on the past or the future.

- Happiness is mental fitness.

- Don't wait for the happy ending.

- Enjoy the journey.

- Do something foolish.

Cool Risk

CHAPTER THREE

WHY WORRY?

Cartoon by Michael Mittag

The F Word

Progress in our quest for happiness involves taking worthwhile risks. Here are some of the risks we might take:

- A mother encourages her child to play outside with other children.

- An old lady goes to visit her friend on the other side of town.

- A young person enrols for a training course.

- A wealthy man makes a donation to fund an orphanage in Africa.

All of these are everyday decisions that offer benefits for the risk taker and for others. However, such opportunities for happiness are often rejected because the risk is seen as too great. Why do we do that? Reasons for avoiding risk can be many and complex. Some of the things that can put people off are unfamiliar circumstances, lack of personal control, overwhelming scale, and threats that are man-made (and therefore seen as unnatural). While these are all relevant, they amount to the same thing. They can be summed up by one word: fear.

- The mother is afraid that harm will come to her child.

- The old lady is intimidated by fear of crime.

- The young person is worried about what friends will think, and the possibility of failure.

- The wealthy man is afraid that his money will be used in ways he cannot control.

Some people don't like to use the word 'fear' for this kind of risk aversion. There are two main reasons: one is that fear is focused and the other is that fear can be healthy.

Fear is focused. Fear is a response to a real threat, such as somebody pointing a gun at you. In this case the fear has a focus – the gun or the person with the finger on the trigger. A vague fear of gun crime, when you have never experienced it, is a different kind of fear, which is perhaps better described as worry or anxiety.

Fear is healthy. Fear is a natural response that is essential for survival. A world without fear would be impossible. Imagine, for example, being in a car with a driver who is completely fearless. Now imagine that you, and all the other people on the road, also have no fear. Nobody would last long!

The pervasive, unfocused fear that we usually call worry or anxiety causes unhappiness. This is not just because the feeling itself is unpleasant. It also prevents us from taking the very risks that could bring about the benefits we want.

NO FEAR

Fear is not worth being scared of
Just something you should be aware of.
Otherwise, it's no fun
And you get nothing done –
Like headlights you're stuck in the glare of.

Don't Panic!

The BBC sitcom *Dad's Army* is classic British comedy. It was originally shown on TV between 1968 and 1977. Repeats are still popular around the world in places where British humour is appreciated. The continuing popularity is surprising for a show set in war time – with a cast that is mostly male and elderly

– and a title sequence that includes three swastikas! One of the things about *Dad's Army* that helps its enduring appeal is the gentle satire. It allows us to laugh at our foibles and fears. The excitable Corporal Jones yells 'Don't panic!' in a way more likely to cause panic than prevent it. Private Frazer intones, 'We're doomed', in his famously spooky voice. Sergeant Wilson simply rolls his eyes and murmurs, 'Do you think that's wise, Sir?'

Each character, in his own way, is doing what we all do in real life, which is to spread fear and doubt like a plague. This is natural. Animals do it too. We just need to be aware of it so that we can guard against it when it is not helpful. The word 'panic' was originally used to mean 'mysterious'. So 'panic fear' was a kind of fear that was unfocused and unknown, like noises in a forest. Today, panic is an irrational fear. It typically refers to fear that is caused simply by other people being afraid. It is closely associated with worry and anxiety.

Because this kind of fear is spread from person to person, it depends on a group or society for it to increase or decrease. This means that tolerance of certain types of risk can depend on culture. Nuclear power is a good example. In Britain, during the 1970s and 1980s, nuclear power became the Big Bad Wolf. Before construction could start on Sizewell B, the last nuclear power station to be built, there was a four-year public enquiry. All the other nuclear stations are elderly and will be shut down by 2023. If no new ones are built, Sizewell B will be the only nuclear plant left operating in Britain, generating less than 3% of the country's electricity.

Meanwhile, in neighbouring France, they built over 50 nuclear power stations in 20 years. France did not completely escape the wave of anti-nuclear sentiment that swept across Europe, but positive feelings outweighed negative ones. Almost 80% of France's electricity is now generated from nuclear. France is a world leader in nuclear technology and exports electricity to several neighbouring countries, including Britain. In 2008, EDF (*Électricité de France*) took over British Energy, the company that operated most of the British nuclear plants. It seems likely that Sizewell B will not be alone after all.

Opposition to nuclear power decreased in many countries at the start of the 21st century. This was not so much because the Big Bad Wolf had become any less frightening, but because we found something else to be scared of: global warming. The earth was getting warmer and we were afraid we might be causing it. When we started to worry about carbon footprints we took another look at the Big Bad Wolf. Oh yes, we were still afraid of his great big teeth and all that scary stuff – but such dainty feet! Nuclear power has a smaller carbon footprint than solar panels.

Then came Fukushima. In March 2011, an earthquake and tsunami in Japan damaged a nuclear power station. The reactor went out of control, leading to the world's worst nuclear accident since Chernobyl in 1986. The Fukushima disaster – together with waning public awareness of global warming – caused a new wave of anti-nuclear opinion. Specifications were tightened on nuclear stations, even in places that are not prone to earthquakes or tsunamis. The German government announced the complete closure of the country's nuclear industry.

The Germans hope to build up their use of renewable energy such as wind and solar. Meanwhile, they will have to buy electricity from their French neighbours, who show little sign of losing their faith in nuclear power.

PANIC FEAR

With so many things taken care of
I want something new to be scared of –
A fate to appal
And threaten us all –
Ideally, completely unheard of.

Mental Health

Mental health usually means the opposite of what it says. In the same way as 'life insurance' is really about death, 'mental health' is usually more about illness. The Mental Health Foundation is a British charity that tries to focus on being well instead of being ill. The charity published a report in 2009 called *In the Face of Fear*, which included the results of a survey of attitudes to fear.

The survey shows that British people have become more fearful in recent years. Levels of fear have increased in the general ('healthy') population and anxiety disorders have become more common. We try to avoid risk so that we can avoid fear. In the survey, 29% of people said that fear and anxiety have stopped them from doing things they wish they had done. The report says:

> We see ourselves and/or others as vulnerable, try to combat that sense of vulnerability by controlling and restricting risk rather than facing our fears, which in turn makes our fears seem bigger and more unmanageable.

By avoiding risk whenever possible, people become less able to cope with it when it does have to be faced. In a life sheltered from death, poverty and hunger, people are more afraid of these things, not less.

Mental health is a spectrum. There is a big difference between those who are flourishing and those who are clinically ill. There is no clear dividing line between the well and the ill. The statistics for mental illness count those who have been diagnosed by a doctor. However, there are many people who have similar feelings and symptoms, but have not been to the doctor. The same words, 'depressed' and 'anxious', are used both to label people with mental illness and to describe people who are well but unhappy.

It is the old question: what is normal? In the case of blood pressure, there is a wide range over the population. Doctors decide that anything between certain limits will be called normal. It is the same with obesity. There is a continuous spectrum of podginess and doctors decide at which point it will be called obesity. So it is with mental illness. People below the line are diagnosed with mental illness. But there are people above the line who are not feeling too good. The report from the Mental Health Foundation refers to this group as 'languishing'. They are on the mental health spectrum, above those who are actually ill but below those who are mentally fit.

Anxiety and depression are not very different from each other. They are often diagnosed together. What they have in common is that it is not clear exactly what is wrong. Sometimes it seems that the person is afraid of unhappiness itself. Antidepressants have certainly helped many people cope with mental illness. But the huge profits made from Prozac are possible by selling them not only to the mentally ill but also to people in the languishing group – and even to healthy people who are just unhappy about not being happy.

LANGUISHING

As a human, he has the ability
To welcome each new possibility.
But having no plans
He just sits on his hands
And wallows in vulnerability.

Anger and Anxiety

The first *Mr. Men* children's books were published in 1971. Over the next few years, Roger Hargreaves wrote – and drew the pictures for – a large collection of *Mr. Men* books. In all, 39 of them were published in his lifetime. They were a huge success, selling in their millions. After Hargreaves' death, his son Adam finished a few books his father had started and also created some new characters. The *Mr. Men* books (and the *Little Miss* companion series) are still loved by children and adults. Many adults fondly recall the books from their childhood: 'Ah yes,' they say, '*Mr. Happy, Mr. Angry, Mr. Nosey…*'. It is remarkable how often people include *Mr. Angry* in their remembered shortlist of *Mr. Men* books.

This is all the more remarkable because there never was a book about *Mr. Angry*. There was, of course, a *Mr. Happy* – everyone knows that. *Mr. Worry* had his own book. So why no *Mr. Angry* when anger is such a common feeling? I don't know, but I suspect it is because anger is not a socially acceptable emotion. It's not nice to be angry. Winston Churchill, who was a famously angry person, often apologised for his outbursts. Nevertheless, he clearly thought anger was an important part of his personality. He is widely quoted as saying, 'A man is about as big as the things that make him angry.'

Fear and anger are the big two – so basic that they are more instinct than emotion. They are the core of the fight-or-flight response. Both feelings cause mental distress and similar physical reactions. Even the words we use for anger and fear – 'anger' and 'anxiety' – come from the same Latin source, meaning 'to strangle'. Funnily enough, the word 'worry' comes from an Old English word that also means 'to strangle'.

Although anger and fear give us similar 'strangled' feelings, there is a very important difference from the point of view of risk taking. They are, in fact, opposites: fight or flight. Fear makes us avoid risks. Anger pushes us to take risks. Does this mean that fear is acceptable, while anger is not? Risk taking is not necessarily bad. Taking risks is the path to many of the genuinely good things in life. If we are strangled by worry, we are inclined to hide or run away instead of facing up to challenges.

Anger is a basic response to injustice. If it spurs us into action it is good, provided the action is not aggressive. Part of the reason why anger has such a bad press is its association with aggression. However, aggression is only one possible response to anger. And aggression can also be a response to fear.

STRANGLED

Driven she was to distraction
Attempting an online transaction.
She threatened the tech
With wringing his neck
But didn't get much satisfaction.

Plucking Up Courage

Long ago, long before the need for happy endings, philosophers recognised two types of thought. They supposed that rational thinking was done in the brain while other crazy stuff – emotions, passions and so on – came from the heart, stomach, gut or other internal organs. This seems weird to us now in an age when brain scanners can practically show our feelings on a computer screen. However, we still recognize the same two types of thought. We still often refer to them as head and heart, even though we know the heart has nothing to do with it.

The ancient philosophy lives on in our language. We talk about heartache, butterflies in the stomach and gut feelings, all of which actually originate in the mind. The phrase 'hearts and minds', which appeared in the *King James Bible*, is still in common use today. We can easily see where the old ideas came from. Sex does make your heart throb. Nerves do make your stomach feel funny. And your bowels tend to behave badly when you're afraid. What we call a gut reaction is not just made apparently without thinking; it is also fast. That's how it is with emotional responses. 'Heart' thinking tends to happen first and then 'head' thinking follows up later – if indeed it kicks in at all.

When facing a risk, fear tends to assert itself before we have time to think coolly about it. After some thought, we might decide it is not so risky after all. More often than not, it still feels scary after thinking about it. If the risk is worth it, then we face the prospect of going ahead even though we still feel afraid. How do we do that? The answer is courage. There is a popular self-help book by Susan Jeffers called *Feel the Fear and Do It Anyway®*. That's what courage is: feeling the fear and doing it anyway. You cannot be courageous unless you are afraid.

Most of us these days don't have much to do with dead bodies. Meat is something that comes in a convenient shape, on a polystyrene tray, wrapped in plastic film. However, people who work in slaughterhouses still use the word 'pluck' to refer to internal organs that are removed from an animal's carcase. So 'pluck' and 'guts' are much the same. By using these terms to talk about courage, our language recognizes it as something deep within us. The word 'courage' itself comes from the Latin for 'heart'.

This deep-seated nature of courage is both good news and bad news. On the one hand, we all have it in us. Hooray! On the other hand, we cannot get it from outside ourselves. Boo! We can only develop it with practice. If we repeatedly give in to fear, then fear becomes normal and we find it harder to take risks. If we manage to overcome fear with courage, then it gradually becomes easier to accept risk.

WEED

I used to be timid and shy
But now I'm determined to try.
I'm showing my mettle
By grasping the nettle –
But hoping for dock weed nearby.

Refreshed by Sorrow and Care

I used to live near Edinburgh in Scotland. From an upstairs window it was possible to see over the Firth of Forth to the Ochil Hills in the distance. However, when I first moved there I had no clue that there was such a view. The weather was so bad that it was months before I knew there was a lake nearby, far less a sight of the Ochils. In due course, my family and I ventured out to explore the foothills – and there discovered Dollar Glen.

Dollar Glen is a ravine, carved out by two rivers: the Burn of Sorrow and the Burn of Care. At the top of the ravine stands the ruin of Castle Campbell. In former times the castle was known as the Castle of Gloom and some say the name of the town of Dollar below derives from the Gaelic word *'doilleir'* meaning gloomy. Nevertheless, this glen of the gloomy names is a delightful place, guaranteed to lift the human spirit.

When we speak about worries, we might be inclined to think that they are not too serious – that they are, after all, nothing to worry about. Sorrows and cares, on the other hand, feel heavier. They sound a bit too close to real suffering. And this brings us back to fear. We are afraid of suffering. Sometimes the fear of suffering can be worse than the suffering itself. It is partly a fear of the unknown. We can be afraid that we will be unable to cope with the pain. As pain increases, a certain level of pain feels worse than the same level as it is decreasing. On the way up, we don't know how bad it will get. On the way down, we know we can stand the pain because we've been there before.

When taking risks, we may have to accept suffering in order to achieve the goal we strive for. Sometimes we do not choose the suffering but it comes anyway. Either way, fear can increase the amount of pain. Studies have shown this is true in the case of childbirth – a common example of a risk that involves pain. The risk is accepted in order to achieve a worthwhile outcome, nothing less than life itself. A woman can reduce the pain of childbirth by controlling her fear. Fear increases the pain. Fear is part of the reason why many women choose a caesarean delivery. In the UK, one quarter of all births are caesareans while in the US the figure is higher. However, caesarean birth is a major operation that also carries risks. If the woman is anxious, it will increase her sensation of pain, both during the operation and afterwards. More interesting still, an anxious birth partner – usually the father – tends to increase the mother's pain, even in the case of a caesarean delivery.

SUFFERING

While pondering Sorrow and Care
It is tempting to think, 'It's not fair!'
In our suffering we cry
And we ask ourselves, 'Why?'
But Sorrow and Care are just there.

Fat Chance

Big lotteries, like *Mega Millions* and *Powerball* in the US and *Euro Millions* in Europe, offer the prospect of huge prize money. But the chances of winning a big-money jackpot are very small. Someone who plays *Euro Millions* every week – in the UK for example – has about the same chance of winning the jackpot as being struck by lightning. For the US lotteries, the balance of risk is worse because the chances of winning the jackpot are lower – and the risk of being struck by lightning is higher! Just look at the statistics: you have more chance of being killed in an accident on the way to buy your lottery ticket than you do of winning the jackpot.

So, why do people buy lottery tickets? Clearly there is more to it than calculating probabilities. Indeed, most people don't care about the probabilities at all. They just enjoy a flutter. Lotteries are more popular among people with low incomes and this can lead to accusations. People accuse the lottery operators of exploiting the poor. They accuse the players of being stupid for betting on such unlikely prospects. The second accusation, at least, is unfair. The players are simply behaving in a normal human way. People are more likely to take risks when their prospects are poor – when they literally have nothing to lose.

Economists don't like this. They hate it when people's behaviour doesn't fit their nice calculations. For many years economists buried their heads in the sand and pretended that everybody would behave sensibly if they could. Economic theory followed entirely rational principles. Then, in 2002, Daniel Kahneman took the Nobel Prize for Economics. The surprising thing was that Kahneman was a psychologist, not an economist. He won the prize for what he called Prospect Theory. In a nutshell, Prospect Theory says this: people with poor prospects are more willing to take risks, whereas people with good prospects are more cautious. The name they gave to this fear of loss was 'loss aversion'.

The more we have, the more we are afraid of losing it, especially if we feel that our wealth was hard earned. Modern affluent societies have, in many ways, never had it so good. We enjoy higher levels of peace, comfort, security and life expectancy. And yet, we seem to be increasingly fearful and lacking in confidence. We are, consequently, reluctant to take risks. This can be explained in part by the loss aversion of Prospect Theory. People are not stupid to feel this way. It is a normal part of being human. However, it can be useful to realize what is going on so that when our fast-acting, emotional and irrational side ('heart') has finished deciding what we are not going to do, we can consult our reason ('head') to get a second opinion.

Using reason to overrule a gut reaction is never easy, nor is it necessarily the best thing to do. One cure for loss aversion would be to give away everything you own. But that feels like an enormous risk.

PROSPECTS IN PRACTICE

The bankers whose prospects are brightening
Find life is increasingly frightening.
They aren't afraid
Of the risks of their trade
But the clients whose belts they are tightening.

Call Security!

As I write this, I have on my desk two books about fear. These books are very different from each other but they have one thing in common. Both books, on the very first page, mention 9/11. The attacks in 2001 on the New York World Trade Center and the Pentagon became an icon of fear and risk. Many people referred to the attackers as terrorists. Shortly after 9/11, President George W. Bush launched his War on Terror. The Reuters news agency, however, refused to use the word 'terrorist' when reporting such events. They are often criticized for this policy. Reuters says they are in the business of facts and not opinions. 'Terrorist' can be an emotive word. It is often said that one man's terrorist is another man's freedom fighter.

When it comes to it, terrorism is as difficult to define as risk. The word has its origins in fear. 'Terror' basically means extreme fear or dread, and it can still be used in that way. But, increasingly, it is reserved to describe violence against civilians that is caused by shadowy rebel groups. The U.S. War on Terror did very little to dispel fear. What it did was cost a fistful of dollars and reduced, not increased, the liberty of the American people.

Anywhere in the world, except for parts of the Middle East, the chance of becoming a victim of terrorism is tiny. It is about as likely as winning the lottery jackpot. However, we all have trouble with small probabilities. Nearly every week somebody hits the jackpot. We see their names and faces. It looks like a common event. It is hard to realize just how unlikely it is to happen to me. Fortunately, terrorist incidents do not happen every week. But they do happen and they are well publicized. It is in the interests of some groups to promote the idea that terrorism is a high risk.

How should we respond to the threat of terrorism? Take, for example, airport security. We put up with a lot of expense, indignity and inconvenience. Does all this seriously reduce the risk? An item in the *British Medical Journal* caught my attention. The article, written in 2007, compared airport security with medical screening such as screening for breast cancer. In order for such a medical programme to be approved, it must provide scientific evidence to justify it. The proposed screening must first of all be effective. The benefits must be balanced against costs and the process must be acceptable to the public. In the case of airport security screening, the researchers were unable to find any such evidence.

The intention of terrorists is presumably to terrify. The paradox is that our response to terrorism often does the terrorists' job for them. We encourage each other to be afraid. We accept high costs and restrictions of liberty in order to combat the perceived threat. We are unable to accept that bad stuff happens. It just does. It is impossible to be completely secure. The search for security is linked to the craving for certainty. The words 'sure' and 'secure' originally had much the same meaning. It is normal to worry about insecurity and uncertainty. They will never go away. We need to find a balance by accepting a reasonable level of risk.

NO FEAR, NO GAIN

In security, business is brisk
For equipment to scan and to frisk.
About power and profit
They want a lot of it
But care a lot less about risk.

Chewing the Cud: Chapter Three

- Worry and anxiety are forms of fear.

- Fear can spread like a plague.

- Anxiety stops us doing what we want to do.

- Anger is opposite to fear when it comes to risk taking.

- Courage is feeling the fear and doing it anyway.

- Controlling fear reduces suffering.

- We need to find a reasonable level of risk.

CHAPTER FOUR

MAKING SENSE

That said, there is always a small non-zero risk left.

We're all gonna die

Cartoon by Michael Mittag

Imagine That!

The human mind is a weird and wonderful creation. We use our imagination to fill in gaps in our knowledge and dress up our memories. Most of the time we do this without even noticing. Psychologists agree that this filling-in process goes on but they have not come up with a name for it. Well, I have the word they need. It was invented many years ago by my four-year-old son.

He noticed, very perceptively, that what his mother was confidently telling him was perhaps not entirely supported by the facts. He looked up at her and said, 'You're prophicating, aren't you.' He said it not accusingly, but more with the air of a student learning a key lesson. The word 'prophicating' has been part of the family vocabulary ever since.

My wife has a vivid imagination and a strong urge to teach. One result of being blessed with these two gifts is she tends to speak about details that she does not actually know. For example, she talks to a friend on the phone and hears about the friend's new dog. Afterwards, when she tells me about the dog, she uses her hands to demonstrate the exact size of the animal even though she has seen it only in her imagination. I have always considered my wife peculiar in this way, but apparently such behaviour is more normal than I thought. We all do it to some extent and most of the time we can't see the join between imagination and reality.

'Prophicating' is an attractive word for the imaginative filling-in process, partly because it is like three other words:

prophesying - speaking words from divine or other inspiration

fabricating - making stuff up, telling lies

pontificating - speaking confidently and dogmatically

So, to prophicate is to speak from the imagination, *believing it to be real*. It sounds bizarre, but it is normal behaviour. We all do it to some extent. Imagination is a basic part of being human. It helps us make sense of the world.

Good leaders are able to imagine a better future. Not only that, they are usually good speakers too. They can speak about their vision in a way that will fire the imagination of their followers. People need a vision of a brighter future to persuade them to accept the risks necessary to achieve it.

When we get to the future, it often looks different from how we imagined it. The new present in which we find ourselves seems less attractive than we thought it would be. On top of that, there is a temptation to think that the old present was better. That is because imagination also plays a role in our memories of the past. The 'good old days' were probably not as good as they seem in our imagination.

TELLING STORIES

My granny is 'long in the tooth'.
The stories she tells of her youth
With that look in her eyes,
Well, they're not really lies –
Just sort of a different truth.

The Way I See It

Use your imagination now. Imagine a beautiful red rose. Picture a bee visiting the flower, busily foraging for nectar. Although both the rose and the bee are imaginary, you can see the whole scene in your mind's eye. What you see depends on your experience of bees and roses. Your experience is different from mine so your mental picture is also different. But we can both see a bee and a rose even though there is nothing really there. We are well aware that we are using the power of our minds to do this.

In the case of looking at a real rose, it is not obvious what mental processing we are doing. We see with our eyes – and they seem quite separate from the brain. We see colours because human eyes are adapted for colour vision. Our eyes have three types of sensor. Basically one type detects red, another green and the other blue. Light from the rose falls on all three types of sensor but the 'red' ones respond the most. They send a big 'red' signal to the brain.

I still see something different from you when we both look at a *real* rose, although not as different as when we simply imagined it. Our eyes are not the same and they give different signals to our brains. The brain then tries to make sense of the signals that are presented to it. The whole process of colour perception is complex and varies from person to person.

What about the bee? How does she see the rose? Well, for a start, it is not red. Bees, like humans, have three types of colour sensors in their eyes. But, unlike humans, bees cannot see the colour we call red. Instead, their eyes are sensitive to colours at the other end of the spectrum, in the ultraviolet range. We don't have names for these colours because we can't see them. The rose has some interesting information for the bee that we can't see.

What all this means is that the redness of the rose is not so much a feature of the rose itself as an effect of the way we see it. There is, in a very real sense, more to the rose than meets the eye. It is like that with all our senses: sight, touch, taste, smell and hearing. The senses themselves detect what goes on in our surroundings and pass signals to the brain, which attempts to make sense of it all. Very often the brain has to rely heavily on imagination, based on experience.

The brain is amazingly adaptable. I experienced this myself, getting used to varifocal lenses in my glasses. People can get used to even stranger things. Experiments have been done with people wearing special glasses or electronic headsets that turn the world upside down. After several days in an upside-down world, the brain could make sense of it. Victims were able to move about and act almost normally. (Although it is difficult to act *completely* normally wearing a weird headset!) After removing the upside-down glasses, the victim needed only a few hours to regain normal vision.

It is even possible for the brain to replace one sense with another. Some blind people have been helped by devices that convert images to sounds. The blind person is able to enjoy a limited visual experience by listening to sounds through headphones. Brain scans have shown that what the blind person 'sees' is being processed by the part of the brain that normally deals with vision.

SEEING AS HOW IT IS

We can never quite see eye to eye
And it's easy to understand why.
You can't ascertain
What goes on in my brain.
And for that matter, neither can I.

Trouble with Relatives

So how much are we making stuff up and how much are we just making sense of reality? The evidence suggests that we are not really bothered about absolute truth. Our system of perception is more to do with relative values. Take a look at this popular illusion by Edward Adelson:

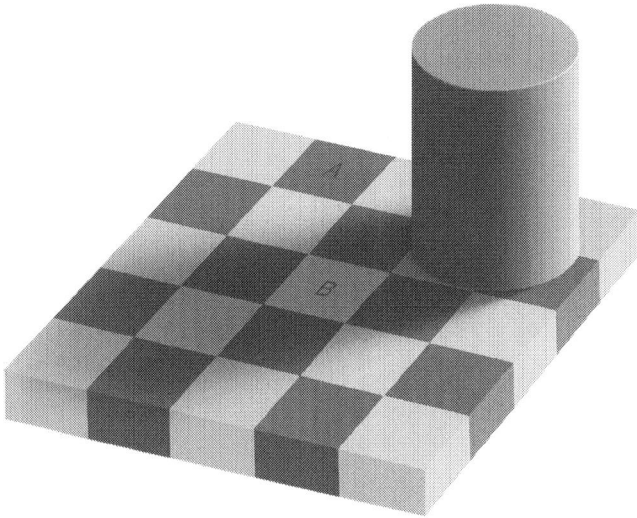

In this image, the squares labelled A and B are identical. They are exactly the same shade of grey. And yet we see a checkerboard of black and white squares in which A is black and B is white. It is quite hard to believe they are the same. The illusion exploits several aspects of the way we see things but the main one is relativity. Square A is surrounded by much lighter squares, making it look dark. Square B is surrounded by much darker squares, making it look light. This is not a weakness or malfunction of the brain, exposed by a clever illusion. It is an illustration of how wonderful the brain is. This is a case of the brain doing what it is good at – making sense of some complex and confusing input.

We are more sensitive to differences than to absolute values. For a warning signal, a flashing light is better than a steady one. This relativity applies to all our senses, not just to sight. An audible warning is usually a rising-and-falling wail or an intermittent beep; think of a police siren or a big vehicle reversing. The same with taste: an orange might be sweet but it tastes sour if eaten immediately after a jam sandwich.

It is not just our physical senses. Relativity also applies to more abstract perception – such as happiness. Think of the squares on the checkerboard as separate days. Square A is a day in a brighter part of life. It is surrounded by some really happy days and therefore seems unhappy by comparison. Square B is a day in the shadows. However, because it is surrounded by darker days, it seems a happy day. If it were possible to look at the two days objectively, they would seem equally happy. But that's not how we see things.

SPOT THE DIFFERENCE

I thought it was change that I feared,
Recoiling from anything weird.
But the thing that was strange
When I got rid of change
Was that everything else disappeared.

How Can I Put This?

Tabloid newspapers are fond of headlines like *"Maniac Kills Mum"*. Sometimes, for variety, they might replace *maniac* with *psycho* or *fiend*. Stories like this play on people's fear of mental disorder to sell newspapers. This is unfortunate. The statistics simply do not support the idea of a high risk of violence at the hands of the mentally ill. The sad fact is that people with mental illness are far more likely to be *victims* of violent crime.

Society wants to control violent behaviour. So doctors are asked to assess mental patients and make a judgement about whether they are likely to be violent. Patients might be put in hospital against their will, so it is a serious issue for patients as well as for society. The doctors have been given a very difficult task. The risk of violence is so low that it is impossible to make a reliable judgement with the amount of information normally available.

In one study, a group of doctors was asked to assess a number of mental patients to determine how dangerous they might be. The doctors were given the patients' case notes and asked to rate the patients on a scale, like SCALE A below. For each patient they were asked to circle one of the numbers to answer the question: 'Out of 100 patients with these symptoms, how many will be violent?'

SCALE A

0	10	20	30	40	50	60	70	80	90	100

Another group of doctors was given the same task as the first group. But this second group was given a different rating scale, like SCALE B below. This scale has more options to distinguish between low-risk patients. It has no possibility to distinguish between high-risk patients (the highest category being 'greater than 40').

SCALE B

0	1	2	5	10	15	20	25	30	40	>40

The results of the study were fascinating. Doctors using SCALE A found the patients to be at a high risk of violent behaviour. Those using SCALE B found the same group of patients to be low risk. However, the relative assessment of one patient compared to another was consistent, whether they were assessed on SCALE A or SCALE B. The doctors used the two scales in exactly the same way – but as if they contained no numbers at all!

The doctors were unable to make a reliable assessment of absolute risk. So they followed their human preference for relativity. They did this without being aware of it. They did this even when they were warned about it before starting the exercise. They couldn't help it! The same thing happens with the checkerboard illusion. When you know that A and B are identical – and have some explanation – they still don't look the same.

The doctors found it hard to rate the mental patients because there was a lot of uncertainty. They did not have enough information to make a reliable decision. In such a case, the decision is influenced by the way the information is presented. This is how it is with risk. If there is no uncertainty, there is no risk. Risky decisions are always based on incomplete information. Look carefully at the way the information is presented to see if it biases the decision one way or another.

GOING ROUND AND ROUND

When weighing the chance of a win
It's hard to know where to begin.
It's such a frustration
When good information
So often turns out to be spin.

Well, What Did You Expect?

A funny thing happened to me at Basel Airport. It involved one of those moving walkways. You know the kind of thing – like an escalator, but flat. As I approached it, I could see it was not moving and most people were avoiding it. I decided to walk along it anyway. As I stepped onto it, I stumbled. 'Aha!' I thought, 'How interesting. My brain was expecting the walkway to be moving. So it tried to allow for the movement, which caused me to stumble because the walkway was not actually moving.' When I reached the other end of the walkway, I was ready for it. I stepped carefully off the stationary walkway onto the stationary floor. I stumbled! Even though I was prepared for it, I could not counteract what my brain was doing.

Feelings about anything – including happiness and risk – are strongly affected by expectations. If I tell a client the job will be completed in a week – and it actually takes two weeks – the client is unhappy. If I said the job will take three weeks, the client is delighted when it is done in two. When a company publishes bad financial results, its shares can go up on the stock market. This is usually because the results, although bad, are not as bad as the market expected. In the high-risk environment of the stock market, expectation is everything.

The checkerboard illusion is reinforced by what we expect to see. The regular checkerboard pattern of black and white squares is one we easily recognize. Once the pattern is registered, we expect to see a black square in certain positions and a white square in the others. Square A looks dark and Square B looks light partly because of their positions in the overall pattern.

The same four-year-old who came up with the word 'prophicating' used to say his prayers before going to bed. He would begin, 'Thank you for peas'. This was a puzzle to his parents, who knew he was not really fond of green vegetables. After some time, we realized he was referring to 'peace', something he knew they prayed about at church. He was doing what we all do. He was turning a strange thing into a familiar one. 'Peace' turned into the nearest thing known to him, which was 'peas'.

Expectation is about what you know. Therefore, the concept of expectation is not far away from average, usual or everyday. There is a term used in statistics and probability theory called 'expectation', which is a kind of average. We expect things to be normal. This is part of the difficulty with expectations. Because they are so average, so humdrum, we hardly notice them. We have expectations we are not aware of.

'Managing expectations' is one of those phrases that have leaked out of the business world into everyday life. Although I hate most of them, this one I quite like. It describes the process of dealing with unrecognized expectations. It is not simply about telling clients three weeks so that they are happy with two. It is that, but much more. It is about discovering – and meeting – the unspoken expectations. This is valuable, not just in business, but in all kinds of relationships.

When I was a child, my mother always carved the meat. My father, in fact, had very little to do with food apart from eating it. In my wife-to-be's household, it was the other way round. Her father did the carving. He guarded it as his special privilege and obviously enjoyed the task. When we were married, neither of us expected to carve meat – and we didn't have the skill to do so. It was not something we had thought about beforehand. I'm not saying this is something that would have made us cancel the wedding. But it is always worth trying to understand other people's expectations – and our own.

EXPECTATION

Heaven had seemed in his reach
When she asked him for Sex on the Beach.
But he hadn't inquired
Whether what she desired
Was a cocktail that tasted of peach.

Chicken and Egg

After the 2008 US election, the following comment appeared on a website dedicated to US political commentary:

> Obama's victory in the general election was aided by his tremendous fundraising success.

And in another place on the same website:

> Despite raising four times more than her incumbent opponent, Republican Deborah Honeycutt lost this week by a landslide in the race to represent Georgia's 13th District.

Obama raised less than twice as much funding as his opponent and he *won* by a landslide. Honeycutt raised four times as much as her opponent and she *lost* by a landslide. And yet the commentators believe that money helped Obama to win.

What's going on here? Obama spends a load of money on his campaign and wins. People make the cause-and-effect link that seems obvious. They believe what they want to believe. But there is not much evidence for it. First of all, there have been plenty of political candidates who spent a lot of cash and lost. Then there is the research carried out by the economist, Steven Levitt, which he wrote about in his book *Freakonomics*. His evidence suggests that the popular belief about campaign spending is a myth.

Of course, Obama's fund-raising success and his election victory were linked. But one was probably not caused by the other. More likely that both were caused by another phenomenon: his popularity!

It is hard to prove whether two observations are cause and effect, have a common cause – or are just coincidences. The debate over possible health effects of overhead electric power lines has rumbled on for some 30 years. A study in Switzerland, for example, found a link between dementia and living near power lines. However, several of the risk factors for dementia also apply to people living in poorer areas. Power lines tend to be found more in poorer areas. So it's more likely that poverty – and not power lines – is a risk factor for dementia. It is human nature to look for explanations. When facing problems, we look for something to blame, or someone – even ourselves if necessary. So when misfortune strikes, and there's an elephant in the room, we blame the elephant.

It is easy to find examples of this phenomenon. A teenager takes a drug for his severe acne. Soon after stopping the medication, the young man kills himself. His parents blame the drug. There is no proof that one caused the other. Many young men commit suicide without having taken powerful acne medication. Global warming is another example. The generally accepted theory is that mankind is warming the globe by releasing carbon dioxide and other stuff into the atmosphere. We are pretty sure about the observations. The average global temperature is going up. The amount of carbon dioxide in the atmosphere is increasing spectacularly. Does one cause the other? That's a lot harder to prove.

TWO WRONGS

A nutty professor in Spain
Has a theory umbrellas cause rain.
In the hills, in his folly,
He puts up his brolly
And rolls it away in the plain.

Too Much of a Good Thing

Taking a risk involves the possibility of losing something of value. But we still take risks – and we need to take risks – because that way we get the chance of gaining something of greater value. It's a trade-off that is not easy to make. Weighing up probabilities is hard and we know we are bad at this. What we find it harder to recognize is that we are also not good at weighing up values.

Value can be something that is clearly defined, like the cost of a lottery ticket or the value of the prizes. Often it is harder to pin down: for example, how do you measure recognition and respect? Value is subjective. It means different things to different people. What *you* value is not the same as what *I* value. More than that, the value of something to you today can be different tomorrow. (This type of personalized value is what risk analysts usually call 'utility', but I'll stick with 'value'.)

The value of food is a striking illustration. One billion people in the world do not have enough to eat. At the same time, one and a half billion people are overweight. Compare the value of food in each case. How many calories are there in a cream bun or a cream cheese bagel? Let's say about 300. Think about the value of those 300 calories to a starving person. The value of the same 300 calories to an obese person is far less, probably negative.

Anything can be poisonous if you get too much of it – even water. Water is not just good for you, but essential for life. You can't survive long without water. When you are thirsty, a drink of water has great value. When you're not thirsty, the water doesn't do you any more good. At this point, people usually stop drinking. But if you keep on drinking to excess, it can kill you. I'm not talking about contaminated water. Even good clean water can be lethal in large quantities.

Seeing value as something relative also applies to things that are hard to measure. Most people want recognition and respect. It is good to know that your boss appreciates your work. It is reassuring to hear a kind word from a family member. Although we can't measure these things we usually feel that we can't get enough of them. But when people become famous, they realize it's possible to have too much of this good thing. After a while they long to walk down the street unnoticed.

It's not black and white: one moment something is good and then suddenly it's bad. No, it's not like that. It is a continuous spectrum. When you have nothing, a small prize has great value. As you get more, the same size of prize has less value. Something for which you were prepared to take a big risk now seems less worthwhile. As you get still more, you are no longer willing to take a risk for what now seems a small prize.

SATISFACTION

A lack of essentials is tough
And so is a surfeit of stuff.
But it's hard to decide
That the brakes be applied
The moment enough is enough.

Don't Even Think About It

St. Andrews in Scotland claims to be the home of golf. Ann Arbor in the US state of Michigan also has a reputation for fine golf courses. No surprise, then, that researchers at the University of St. Andrews and the University of Michigan should work together on a project about golf. More surprising is what they discovered. They found that golfers lost their skill by describing it.

A mix of skilled golfers and novices were tested in a putting exercise. After the test, half of them were asked to spend five minutes describing what they had done. The other half spent five minutes doing a verbal exercise nothing to do with golf. Then everyone did the putting test again. The novices were mostly unaffected. The skilled golfers were reduced to the level of novices!

My father was a good driver and he taught me to drive. He found it hard to explain exactly how to work the pedals in such a way that the vehicle moves off smoothly. We are all familiar with the idea of an expert who is unable to pass on his expertise. Think of a university professor who can't teach. However, the golf research is about something different. It is about losing a skill simply by thinking about it.

When I was a child, I learned to play a few simple pieces on the piano. After a great deal of repetition, I could play them quite fluently. But when I stumbled, and tried to think how to proceed, I got stuck. It was very frustrating. The more I thought about it, the harder it was to play. This is like the golfers who put their golf play into words. An established skill is hard to recall by deliberate thinking.

Malcolm Gladwell gives several examples of this phenomenon in his book *Blink: the Power of Thinking without Thinking*. An expert is likely to make a better judgment by taking a quick decision instead of thinking about it and discussing it. The reason seems to be that expertise – the skill of an expert – is complex and hard to describe. Once the expert puts it into words, there is a risk of concentrating on only those parts of the skill that can be described. A whole range of other hard-to-describe factors are neglected – and it is these subtle factors that really set the expert apart from the novice.

What does this say about the management of skilled workers who are asked to justify what they are doing at every stage? How much can we rely on the opinion of a panel of medical experts who debate at length before making their pronouncements? Novices are novices and had better think carefully. But experts should perhaps get on with doing what they are good at and not think about it too much. Taking action without thinking too carefully feels risky but it can be the better option. Believe in your strengths and go for it!

TRUST ME, I'M AN EXPERT

I'm an expert so go with the flow
Because studies consistently show
If I spell out for you
What I'm planning to do
I might become less of a pro.

Chewing the Cud: Chapter Four

- We use imagination to fill gaps in our knowledge and memory.

- The way we see things is subjective and personal.

- We are more sensitive to differences than absolute values.

- We are more sensitive to differences even when we think we are not!

- The way we feel about something depends on what we expected.

- It can be hard to distinguish between cause and effect.

- Value means different things to different people.

- Go with your gut feeling – but only if you know what you're doing!

Cool Risk

PART TWO

GETTING TO COOL

CHAPTER FIVE

SHARING

Good risk communication:

As captain of this flight, I deeply regret having to inform you that we are about to crash.

Cartoon by Michael Mittag

Topsy-Turvy Thinking

South Africans have a cute way of referring to almost everything and everybody by a nickname. Edith Lourens was known to her friends as Topsy. During the Second World War, Topsy met an English serviceman who was stationed in South Africa. After the war, she moved to England to marry her wartime sweetheart. She died at a ripe old age, having lived over 60 years in England. And yet, whenever Topsy used the expression 'at home' she was always talking about South Africa.

When I married Topsy's daughter, I found it hard to fit mother-in-law's fond memories of 'home' with the current news from South Africa. The *apartheid* system had been imposed not long after Topsy left South

Africa. TV pictures from 'home' showed only injustice and oppression. Where were all the lovable characters with bizarre nicknames? I assumed that they lived on only in Topsy's reminiscences.

Then Nelson Mandela was released after 27 years in jail. *Apartheid* was crumbling. Suddenly, it was thinkable to visit South Africa. Before long I was there with my wife and two teenage sons. What a wonderful country! And yes, there they were – the family! I got to know my wife better by visiting South Africa and she understood herself more deeply after spending time with her relatives. One particular cousin made a lasting impression on us both. His parents' farm could not support him and his family so he set up his own business – making coffins! It was a shrewd decision. There was, and still is, a big market for coffins in South Africa.

While in South Africa, we planned to go hiking along the Wild Coast of the Transkei, a region known for its outstanding natural beauty – and its violence. South African relatives and their (white) friends were horrified. We would surely be murdered, or robbed at the very least! They were even more aghast when they realized that we intended to travel to the Wild Coast on local public transport – the 'black buses'. But did that stop us? The four members of my family attracted a lot of attention as the only white people on the buses. And I have to admit that it *was* a somewhat tortuous journey. When there were no more buses, we walked. We were able to hitch rides on some of the few vehicles that chanced along. One moment, we were bouncing around in the back of an empty army truck. The next, we were in the back of a pick-up, perched precariously on crates of soft drinks.

I was no way a seasoned hitchhiker. My introduction to hitchhiking had been earlier in that same African trip. We were in Zimbabwe. We had taken a bus from Bulawayo to the Hwange National Park and it turned out that the bus stop was 24km from the park centre! We started walking but were soon picked up by a pick-up. It was a somewhat dilapidated vehicle and the driver took frequent swigs from a bottle of beer. But it was great! The driver went out of his way to take us where we wanted to go – and even pointed out wildlife on the way. Were we taking a risk? You bet. But the choice was easy: a risky ride with a beer-swilling guide or a 24km hike through the game park!

In spite of our hitchhiking adventures in Africa, we got home safe and sound. We were not murdered, robbed or molested in any way. The only people we met were friendly and helpful. We also escaped the more likely fate of being killed in a road accident!

SAFARI SO GOOD

A culture corrupted by worry
Thinks: 'Better be safe, than sorry'
But sorrow exists
In the chances we've missed.
Life is a super safari!

The Hitchhiker's Guide

How risky is hitchhiking? When I tried it with my family in Africa we came to no harm. Were we just lucky? Nobody knows. Very few serious studies have looked at the risks of hitchhiking. There is no reliable data. So nobody knows. Everything about hitchhiking is uncertain.

When there is uncertainty, we rely on our feelings. And, in the case of hitchhiking, the strongest influence is culture. Hitchhiking, from the beginning, has been seen in most western societies as somewhat offbeat. A person standing by the side of the road with thumb extended – and no broken-down vehicle nearby – has always been seen as a bit weird. But the cultural story has changed over the years. In the 1970s, weird was unconventional but also amusing and interesting. At the start of the 21st century, weird is threatening and dangerous.

It's not just the motorists who fear for their own safety. The budget traveller is afraid that a driver might turn out to be a rapist or murderer. The driver, who has no such intentions, is afraid of being accused of assault. Everyone is afraid of everyone else. The sociologist Frank Furedi has long lamented the growing culture of fear in western societies. In the preface to his book *Culture of Fear Revisited*, he writes:

> When I started working at my university all my students used to hitchhike to get into town or travel further afield. I would frequently see queues of 20-25 animated students waiting for a ride. Today, none of them hitches a ride.

Ken Welsh wrote *Hitch-Hiker's Guide to Europe* in 1971. (It was this quirky travel guide that inspired the title of Douglas Adams' even quirkier sci-fi comedy *The Hitchhiker's Guide to the Galaxy*.) There were many new editions of *Hitch-Hiker's Guide to Europe* – almost one every year at first. This was clear evidence of the popularity of the guide and, indirectly, the popularity of hitchhiking. But the new versions became less frequent as the years went by. The 17th edition, which appeared in 1996, turned out to be the last.

There are many reasons for the demise of the *Hitch-Hiker's Guide to Europe* and the decline of hitchhiking itself. We can't blame everything on the rise of the risk society. Travel information is easily available on the internet, which also offers a more interactive experience than a guide book. Travellers are generally not so hard up and there are more opportunities for budget travel. There are still many hitchhikers around. There are even websites for hitchhikers. Nevertheless, there are definitely fewer people prepared to take the risk of riding with a complete stranger.

There is no denying that the decline in hitchhiking is partly due to our cultural perception. There is no reliable evidence that hitchhiking is any more dangerous than it was in the 1970s. But today we tend to see other people – and especially strangers – as inherently risky. It becomes harder, the less normal interaction we have with others. If we are scared of letting children play outside and socialize with other children, is it any wonder that they grow up to be fearful of other people?

TAKEN FOR A RIDE

It's easy to think someone weird –
Their clothing, behaviour or beard.
That strangers are strange
We are not going to change
But they don't always have to be feared.

Culture Shock

I grew up in England and that was all I knew until the age of 20. My first adventure into another country was a trip to France with my girlfriend. We soon discovered new cultural experiences, like the French reaction to kissing in public. People would call or whistle when they spotted us in a public embrace. Passing motorists would sound their horns. I never knew why. I couldn't decide whether their behaviour was due to Catholic disapproval or Gallic *joie de vivre*. Whatever it was, it was a very different culture from at home. The English, whatever they privately thought about public kissing, pretended not to notice.

Many years later, I have travelled widely and lived in several different countries. The biggest culture shock for me remains my first big move, from England to Scotland. As a typical Sassenach, I thought of Scotland as a hilly bit of England – with monsters. This naïve view was quickly shattered as I discovered many cultural differences. One was to do with tea. Many Scots drink it without milk – pretty shocking to an Englishman! I had always drunk my tea with milk. However, being a daring risk-taker, I decided to try it black. I soon found out I liked it better without milk. Before long, I couldn't stand the taste of milky tea.

I still drink tea without milk. Because of this outlandish tea-drinking habit, I am regarded as strange in almost every English household. There is no logic behind it. There is no good reason why milk should be required in tea. I think it makes the tea taste horrible. The blogger 'lynneguist' – an American living in England – wrote on her blog:

> My thinking is that if milk and tea were suited to each other, then tea ice cream would be at least as popular as coffee ice cream. But it isn't, is it?

This is how culture works. There is no good reason for milky tea but everyone (in England) thinks it normal. I am weird because I don't take milk in my tea. In some places it can be hard to get a cup of tea with no milk in it.

Generally speaking, people don't even realize that they do things for cultural reasons. A survey of 5000 English adults asked them to name things they thought were uniquely English. It wasn't a scientific study. The survey was carried out by a beer company and 'a love of pubs' came out top of the list! However, it is interesting that their top 50 included many things that are not particularly English. And it left out some very English things – like putting milk in tea!

Culture has a big influence on our attitude to all kinds of things and that includes risk. This is not surprising. The word 'culture' basically means having an influence. Agri*culture* is about growing stuff in fields instead of foraging in the wild. It's about taking control. Cultural influence can take different forms: peer pressure; social networking; family expectations. It is not just different countries that have different cultures. Any group, large or small, can have its own culture. A gang member may be ready to take particular risks because of the gang's culture. A culture of risk at a bank might lead an investor to adopt particularly risky practices.

It is often the case that we don't realize we are following a culture. We feel we are making a free choice when we have, in fact, been cultivated!

I WOULDN'T DO A THING LIKE THAT

I take quite a rational view
So I feel like a fool (as you do)
When a rule that I swallowed
And slavishly followed
Turns out to be just a taboo.

Mind the Gap

Claude Shannon was an electrical engineer, mathematician, inventor and juggler. He analyzed juggling mathematically. He even built juggling robots. His masterpiece was a tiny stage on which three clowns juggled 11 rings, eight balls and seven clubs – with every moving piece rotating and landing correctly! He said, at the age of 67, 'I've spent lots of time on totally useless things'.

He certainly had some fun. But not everything Shannon did was 'totally useless'. In 1948, he published *A Mathematical Theory of Communication*. In his opening remarks he said something about extending the existing theory. Shannon was being modest. His statistical approach was radically different from anything that had gone before. It created the new science of information theory. Shannon's idea was that any information (speech, pictures, music, etc.) could be broken down into basic elements he called bits. He talked about information flow in bits per second. The principles of digital communication that he invented are used by many things we now take for granted: computers, CDs, mobile phones and the internet, to name just a few.

Shannon's achievement ranks alongside Newton's laws of motion, Darwin's theory of natural selection and Einstein's theory of relativity. In Shannon's statistical theory, information flow depends on uncertainty – on surprise. It seems obvious with hindsight: if the recipient knows in advance what the message will be, there is no communication!

The Latin word for 'sharing' gave us the word 'communicate'; also 'commune' and 'community'. Culture – at least in the sense that it affects risk – is about the things we share as a community. Culture puts a spin on any information received. We tend to accept things that reinforce our culture and reject things that go against it. We stick to what we know. Communicating with people of a different culture is a challenge. Much has been written about it. Much has also been written about risk communication. But it is not generally recognized that most risk communication is cross-cultural.

The phrase 'cross-cultural communication' usually refers to sharing between countries or ethnic groups. However, every community has its own culture – its particular customs, values and language. When a nuclear risk analyst speaks to an environmental activist there is a cultural divide. It is not that either of them is more risk averse than the other, just that they see things differently. The nuclear engineer believes that nuclear power is a risk worth taking, but may be horrified at the thought of hitchhiking anywhere. The environmental activist is appalled by the whole idea of nuclear engineering, but thinks nothing of hitchhiking to demonstrations. Real communication between the two cultures is a challenge.

When people within a group talk to each other, a lot of what they say serves to strengthen their group identity. They use jargon, abbreviations and 'in' phrases that can only be understood by group members. Such language helps to establish a speaker's status as a member of the group. It also helps to keep non-members on the outside. It does little to inform members about the world outside the group – which is most of the world. A cool attitude to risk needs a wider understanding of the world. More openness. A readiness to be surprised.

SHANNON'S LAW?

An obdurate urge to excel
Often ends on the highway to hell.
No achievement's enough
'Cause it helps to do stuff
That is totally useless as well.

Getting the Message

Many people involved in risk communication complain about the media. They get annoyed and frustrated when their carefully prepared statistics are distorted beyond recognition. However, we should pause for thought before being too ready to criticize the media. Journalists are not usually risk specialists. Education of the audience is not their primary concern. Indeed, most of the audience is not seeking to be educated either. They want to be entertained! Editors know that they can get attention by appealing to powerful basic emotions: sex; fear; a mother's concern for her child; a man's defence of his territory. There is no room here for complicated statistics. A sensational personal story, complete with pictures, makes for much better television.

I got this old by rigorously avoiding all risks.

And I can tell you all about it.

In two minutes flat.

Cartoon by Michael Mittag

The story of the MMR vaccine controversy is a classic risk thriller. It began in 1998 when the medical journal *The Lancet* published results of some research done at the Royal Free Hospital in London. The leading author of the article was Dr. Andrew Wakefield. He suggested that autism might be caused by MMR – the triple vaccine for measles, mumps and rubella (German measles). The story was picked up by the general media. Some newspapers saw it as an opportunity to campaign against the government. The scare was on. More and more parents chose not to have their children vaccinated. As a result, the number of cases of measles rose dramatically.

As the years went by, the story behind the story gradually emerged. At the time of the original article in 1998, Dr. Wakefield had applied for a patent for a measles vaccine of his own. He was also being paid by lawyers acting in a legal case against three MMR manufacturers. So his career – and his bank balance – would be enhanced if he could discredit the MMR vaccine. But it didn't turn out like that. In 2010,

Wakefield was struck off the medical register (together with another Royal Free doctor) for improper and unethical practices in the original study. *The Lancet* retracted the 1998 article. Wakefield published a book.

There never was any evidence to link MMR with autism. Unfortunately, large numbers of children do develop autism. First signs of it can be seen during the second year of life. This is about the same time as the MMR vaccination is given. Parents who blamed MMR for their child's autism were victims of the cause-and-effect trap – as well as victims of the MMR scare.

What can we say about the role of the media in all this? I don't defend the newspapers who tried to make political capital out of the story. But generally we should expect that a sensational link between a vaccine and autism would be widely reported. What I find harder to accept is the original publication by *The Lancet* of sensational findings that were based on a small and rather dodgy-looking study. Newspapers were doing what they do – selling newspapers. We have to accept that a headline like 'Vaccine causes autism' sells more papers than 'Vaccine probably doesn't cause autism'.

SENSE AND SENSIBILITY
Rather than join the assault
To find everybody at fault,
Try taking the tales
You receive in emails
With sizeable pinches of salt.

Finding Our Way

How do we assess risk? The basic answer is that we try it for ourselves. Think about learning to drink from a cup. As a child, I gradually discovered that, if I put my cup of juice near the edge of the table, I was more likely to knock it over than if it was safely away from the edge. I did not learn this by my mother telling me, 'Don't put the cup there, darling, or you might knock it over.' No, I learned this by covering myself and the dog with fruit juice a few times! We call this process of learning by doing 'experience' – from the Latin *experior* which means 'to try it'.

After a while, I realized that when mother gave me advice, it would be best to take notice. She seemed to know some useful things that could save me from unpleasant outcomes. I trusted her advice. But there comes a time for all of us when we realize that our parents don't know everything after all. Then, if we can't try something for ourselves, we turn to other people who have tried it. We call these people 'experts' – from the past tense of *experior*, meaning 'they tried it'. In simple societies, the old people are the experts. They tried everything. But in a complex society, the elders are no longer the experts. There are just too many things! So the elders didn't get round to trying them all. The trouble is we don't quite know who the experts are any more. An expert in one thing is just like the rest of us when it comes to everything else they haven't tried.

Some years ago I was driving in France. There I am, bowling along the main road to Saint Malo. Then, suddenly and inexplicably, I'm in the town of Caen. *Centre ville*. And I'm lost. I go round and round, trying to escape an inscrutable one-way system. (The French term *'sens unique'* seems particularly appropriate!) I have no choice but to stop and ask directions. Fortunately there's a kind-looking man on the corner who looks as if he is in no hurry to go anywhere. Proudly, I ask him my well-rehearsed phrase-book question: *'Monsieur, comment fait-on pour aller à Saint Malo, s'il vous plait?'* The kindly *monsieur* beams a toothy smile. He understands. But then he releases a torrent of speech not a bit like the French I learned at school. It might just as well be Old Norse. (He also waves his arms about a lot. People do that when they give directions in any culture.) He is the expert. But I am none the wiser for consulting him because we have no common language.

That's how it is when we are not sure what to do – which is most of the time. We go with our feelings or we try to get more information. Usually it's a combination of the two. If I want more information, I first have to identify an expert – someone who has the experience I'm lacking. Then I have to ask the right question. Not only that: I must also be able to understand the answer. The media play an important role but every medium has its limitations. With television, for example, the experts are often well chosen, but as a viewer I don't get to ask the questions. With the internet I can ask the questions – and there's tons of information available – but it can be hard to know who the experts are. And when I find the real expert (on the disease I think I've got, or the travel destination I have in mind) I might not understand the language.

EXPERIENCE

My faith in the 'expert' decreased
When I realized one thing at least.
His name, I decided,
Just means that he tried it.
He isn't some sort of high priest.

Older and Wiser

Articles published in *Neurobiology of Aging* don't normally get wide press coverage. But some research carried out at Duke University did attract attention. It involved scanning the brains of volunteers while they looked at pictures intended to provoke various emotional responses. The volunteers were two groups of healthy women, one aged around 25 and the other aged around 70. The study found that the old brains responded to the pictures in much the same way as the young brains did. However, there were differences in what they made of it. The old brains were better at evaluating and controlling the emotional response.

A risky decision is one that has to be made in a state of uncertainty. Most of the decisions we make are risky in this sense. When we don't have all the facts, we use our emotions to help decide what to do. Sometimes we let our emotions decide even when we do have all the facts.

Wisdom is about getting life in perspective. Elders make better decisions partly because of their greater experience. They may not always have more knowledge these days but they have simply been around longer. Their greater time perspective means they have a better grasp of the probabilities of rare events. They can remember the last big flood in the village – and the time England won the FIFA World Cup. But the Duke research suggests that it is more than this. It seems that the older brain is better adapted to dealing with risky decisions. And that means most decisions.

Since ancient times, elders have tended to be leaders of the community. The word 'senate' comes from the same Latin source as 'senior' and 'senile'. The word 'sheikh' means an old man. Even 'priest' comes from the Greek word meaning an elder. Peter Gabriel, musician and activist, was one of the founders of an independent group of eminent global leaders called *The Elders*. Gabriel said:

> In traditional societies, the elders always had a role in conflict resolution, long-term thinking and applying wisdom wherever it was needed. We are moving to this global village and yet we don't have our global elders.

Lack of respect for elders is often thought of as a modern phenomenon, but this is not the case. There are plenty of examples in *The Bible*. King Rehoboam is one. He got into trouble for rejecting the advice of the elders and following the advice of his peers.

The Greek word for wisdom is *sophia*, personified in ancient times by the goddess *Sophia*. *The Bible* also refers to Wisdom as female. Does this mean that we should consider women to be wiser than men? Perhaps women are better at the long-term thinking? However, studies of risky decision making have found that women are more influenced by emotions and moods than men are. Duke University used women for their brain-scan study but they did not say why. Perhaps it was simply based on the availability of a group of healthy 70-year-olds.

OLD SAYING

Although we proverbialize
About healthy and wealthy and wise.
We strive to be wealthy
And hope to be healthy,
But tend to forget about wise.

Fact or Faith?

On Saturday 22 February 2003, *The Daily Telegraph* carried on its front page a story with the headline: 'Newton set 2060 for end of world'. The story was trailing a BBC TV documentary to be screened the following Saturday. But before the broadcast even went out, the story spread around the world, in newspapers and on the internet. The Canadian academic, Stephen Snobelen – who was quoted in the *Telegraph* story – was overwhelmed by media attention. What caused such a sensation? It was not really that the world might end in 57 years time. Nobody believed that nonsense much anyway. No, the real scandal was that Newton, the father of modern physics, had been involved in biblical prophecy. He was not just involved. He took it very seriously.

This was not news to academics like Snobelen. They were well aware that Newton wrote more about religion than about science. But it was a revelation to the general public, who had been led to believe that science and religion are at odds. Both science and religion are interwoven with culture. Our views on both are affected by the society in which we live. Our behaviour is influenced by what we know and by what we believe – fact and faith. These are two sides of the same coin. Risk is about choices, where we don't know everything. In reality, this means nearly all choices. On one hand, there is what we know – knowledge – that's straightforward. On the other hand, there is how to cope with what we don't know. This is where faith and feelings come into play.

This state of affairs is not something you manage on your own. You share it within your culture. Science is a way of organizing and extending the body of knowledge within a community. Religion is a way of organizing and sharing what we think about the more mysterious experiences. Both sides of the coin are necessary to achieve wholeness. This went without saying to a Renaissance thinker like Newton. He studied and wrote about mathematics and theology without seeing any conflict between them. His religious views were unconventional, as you might expect from a radical thinker. But they were most definitely religious.

Both science and religion shape our attitudes to risk, for better or worse. Both have spurred people on to great achievements. Both have been corrupted for personal gain and political aims. Faith is what drove Mother Teresa of Calcutta to take exceptional risks in order to help the poor of India. But the suicide bomber is also driven by faith (mixed with political idealism). Trust in science encourages people to take risks, even undergoing medical procedures despite the fact they are healthy: for example, vaccination of children against MMR or screening of women for breast cancer. On the other hand, scientific advances are often seen as the cause of many of the risks that society worries about.

People look to science for the certainty they seek. But science does not deliver certainty. Science is an organized way of finding out that there is a lot we don't know. With climate change, for example, it can be hard to see the dividing line between fact and faith. Mathematical modelling has allowed scientists to estimate the rate of global warming. But there is so much that we don't know – and one of the unknowns is what to do about it. Science fails to deliver absolute truth. So people bring their beliefs, politics and cultural bias to the debate. Those who go against the consensus on climate change have been called 'global warming heretics'. The word 'heretic' was used in the past only to condemn people with different *religious* views.

WHAT'S THE MATTER?

Religion and science comparing:
Both can be cruel or caring.
Whether faith you attracts
Or you stick to the facts
I believe it's a matter of sharing.

Chewing the Cud: Chapter Five

- Don't be safe and sorry.

- Resist the growing culture of fear.

- Be aware of how culture affects your behaviour.

- Risk communication has to overcome cultural barriers.

- Make up your own mind and don't shoot the messenger.

- Choose your experts carefully. They don't always know best.

- It might be worth listening to the elders.

- Science and religion both shape attitudes to risk.

CHAPTER SIX

TRUSTING

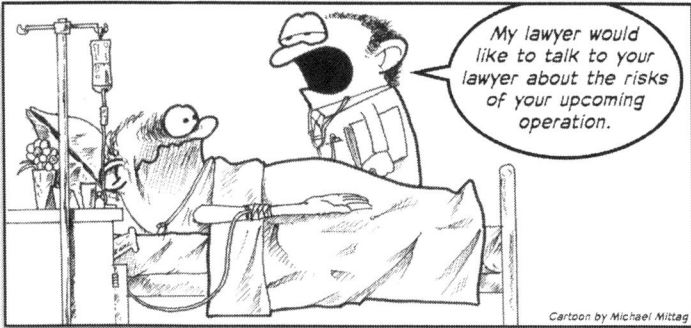

My lawyer would like to talk to your lawyer about the risks of your upcoming operation.

Cartoon by Michael Mittag

The Cuddly Swiss

This tale begins at an Indian restaurant in England. Two men had just enjoyed a good meal with several beers. The bill arrived, but it did not include all the beers that the men had drunk. The man who was paying the bill pointed out the mistake to the waiter and asked for another bill. The waiter seemed surprised but went off to get a new bill. The other guy gently mocked his dining companion for being so morally fastidious.

The man who paid the bill in that Indian restaurant was me. I am not sure I would have been so honest if it had not been for a recent experience in Switzerland. My wife and I had eaten at a restaurant, paid the bill and left. When we got home, I looked at

119

the bill and saw that we had been overcharged. It had not been a good day and it was the last straw to find I had paid for food we had not eaten. The next day, despite my scornful discouragement, my wife took the bill back to the restaurant. They were delighted to see her.

Apparently, they had charged us for some food that had been served to another table. The other customers had noticed the item was missing from their bill and insisted on paying for it. Meanwhile, I had already paid for the same item. The restaurant owners were upset that they had charged two customers for the same food. So they were happy to see my wife the next day and to be able to put it right. Without this Swiss experience, would I have been so honest at the Indian restaurant in England? Or would I have rejoiced in beating the system and getting some free beers?

It seems that Swiss restaurants are a good place to learn about trust. On another occasion, my wife and I had eaten in a country inn. The bill was around 40 Swiss francs and I gave the waitress a crisp, new 100-franc note. After some time, when she had not come back with the change, we went to investigate. We found the woman, flustered and upset, searching everywhere for the note I had given her. She seemed to have put the thing down somewhere and lost it. After several minutes of agitated searching, she went out the back, presumably to speak to the boss. Then she reappeared and started, very despondently, counting out 100-franc notes. When she reached 900 francs and started looking for smaller amounts, I realized she was giving me change from 1,000 francs! She was very relieved when I told her that the 1,000-franc note – which she thought she had lost – never existed.

So I missed out on getting a couple of free beers. Even worse, I missed out on a windfall of 900 Swiss francs (more than 30 good dinners). Does that make me stupid? Did I feel bad about it? The answer to both questions is 'No'. Acting in a trustworthy way makes you feel good. Being trusted gives you a buzz. It's not logical. It's biological. It's all down to the hormone oxytocin. It has been called the 'cuddle chemical' and the 'love hormone'. Although oxytocin has been known since the 1950s, it is only recently that research has linked this hormone to trusting and being trusted. Human society is a complex machine. Oxytocin could well be the oil that stops the machine from seizing up.

OXYTOCIN OVERDOSIN'

Trust me. It will make you feel fine,
A tingling all down your spine.
If you don't get that buzz
Then whatever it does
It will surely make me feel divine.

To Tell You the Truth

When I moved to Switzerland, I didn't know any German. (I discovered that real German speakers don't even say *'Donner und Blitzen'*.) So I went to an evening class called *'Deutsch Intensiv I'*. Like in all language classes, it was not long before we were asked to talk about what we did yesterday, at the weekend or on holiday. It was always hard. I knew what I had been up to, of course, but I didn't know how to say it in German. Eventually, I realized it was easier to pretend. Much easier to think of what I could say in German and talk about that instead of what I had really done. I lied!

Trust is another one of those things that are hard to describe – like risk and happiness. Trust is related to truth. We trust someone if we expect them to speak the truth. At first glance, truth seems to be an easy concept. Something must surely be either true or false? But it's not as clear cut as that. I said earlier that happiness is like a perfect crystal that is all too easily cracked. Truth is like that too. Truth – and trust – is a kind of perfect state that is easily damaged. Just as we speak about being 'unhappy' but not 'unsad', something can be 'untrue' but never 'unfalse'.

True and false are not real opposites. The English language (and it is the same in French and German) reveals some subtle differences in the way we treat these two imposters:

- We speak about 'telling *the* truth' but 'telling *a* lie'. Truth is unique whereas lies can be many.

- There is no single word for communicating the truth. Telling a lie is lying. But telling the truth is not truthing.

- Someone who tells a lie is a liar. There is no word for a person who tells the truth.

This language lesson teaches us that it is easy to lie. but more complex to tell the truth.

There was a time when most people looked to religion for certainty. Priests were trusted, often to extremes. Even if certainty was not the official doctrine, many priests still preached it because that's what people wanted. But then people realized that religion did not have all the answers. Many turned away from religion that could not deliver certainty.

Where did the seekers of certainty turn when they deserted religion? They turned to science. They ignored the fact that many scientific discoveries had much to do with chance. Science has become the modern standard of truth. Scientists themselves know that much of what they do is based on incomplete information. They have to exercise human judgement when they take decisions. This judgement is based on professional experience but it remains uncertain.

Science has in some ways become a religion. Scientific dogmas are defended with religious fervour and opponents are spoken of as heretics. Just as it is unacceptable for a priest to show any doubt, so it is that society does not want to hear the priests of science utter that inconvenient truth: 'I don't know'. Many scientists do honestly try to present the unpalatable uncertainty of their results. However, their message is often distorted by politicians and the media who know that the public does not want truth. Truth is too subtle and complex. People want something plain and simple.

CONSULTING THE ORACLE

Are you sure it is truth that you seek?

Beware 'tis abstruse and unique.

I can tell you a lie

In the blink of an eye

But the truth will take more than a week.

Trust Me, I'm an Actor

On 14 September 2007 there was a run on the British bank, Northern Rock. Customers waited outside the bank, hoping for a chance to withdraw their money. The bank's website went down under the weight of too many people trying to access their accounts. It was the first run on a British bank for 150 years. Many people blamed Robert Peston, the BBC's Business Editor. It was he who broke the news on his blog that the Bank of England had given Northern Rock an emergency loan. Here is an extract from his blog:

> . . . the Chancellor, the Financial Services Authority and the Bank of England don't believe Northern Rock is an unviable business . . . none of us – not even Northern Rock's depositors – probably need to panic that the Bank has had to step in . . .

He was trying to be moderate, although he did use the word 'panic'. There was 'collapse' and 'havoc' somewhere in there too. Anyway, actions speak louder than words, especially where trust is concerned. When depositors saw TV pictures of their fellow customers gathering at the doors of the bank, they knew what they had to do. In two days, £2 billion was sucked out of Northern Rock. The government had to step in and bail it out.

Trust is important in any commercial operation and especially in the financial sector. That's why a bank calls itself Northern Rock: 'Rock' to suggest solidity and 'Northern' to appeal to the loyalty of its customer base in Northern England. But trust is in short supply these days. There is scant respect for many cultural institutions. When the government issues assurances about the safety of investments, people don't trust it. Indeed, something seems risky almost *because* the government declares it to be safe.

If a stage magician announces, 'Here I have an empty box', the audience immediately suspects that the box is not really empty. They will be more ready to believe in its emptiness if the magician simply picks up the box and handles it like it is empty. It is what he does, more than what he says, that earns the trust of the audience. My father used to say, 'Do as I say, not as I do.' (Okay, I may have said it to my own children once or twice too.) But children learn more about values from the behaviour of their parents than by listening to what they say. Doing one thing and saying something different only undermines trust.

Trust is a strange commodity – so hard to build up and so easily lost. Trust is closely allied to risk. One depends on the other. In today's society, risk is shunned and trust is low. Everything feels risky when we trust nobody. Somebody else is always to blame when things go wrong. Marriage is unpopular because it demands too much trust and invites too much risk. In this climate of fear and suspicion, we cannot cope with uncertainty. Government assurances about Northern Rock were not enough for many people, some of whom feared losing their life savings. It was only when the government promised to guarantee all Rock investments – that is, to remove all uncertainty – that the panic subsided.

I DO

Take all those beautiful words
And feed every one to the birds
Because in the long run,
When all's said and done,
Actions speak louder than words.

Getting Your Bearings

In March 2009 Stephen Green made a comment on the crisis in the banking industry. Green was chairman of HSBC, the largest private bank in the world, and also an Anglican priest. This is what he said:

> Underlying all these events is a question about the culture and ethics of the industry. It is as if, too often, people had given up asking whether something was the right thing to do, and focused only on whether it was legal and complied with the rules.

What he was saying was nothing new. Back in 2003 James Schiro, head of Zurich Financial Services, wrote:

The recent corporate failures and accounting scandals did not happen because of a lack of detailed rules on corporate governance. They happened because people who were supposed to be responsible had lost their bearings. Nothing can replace sound judgment, ethical behaviour and credible action. These are the fundamental ingredients of trustworthiness.

It is not enough to have rules and make sure that people stick to them. Rules are necessary in a complex society but they do not absolve us, as individuals, from making moral choices. Trust and respect are not earned by following rules and avoiding risks. They come from pursuing ethical behaviour when there are no rules – or even breaking the rules in order to do the right thing.

It goes further. The very fact of having rules tempts people to push the boundaries. A speed limit on the road is a rule. Basically it says, 'Do not drive faster than this'. It is supposed to be a maximum. Drivers are expected to use their judgement and drive at a speed lower than the limit depending on the road, weather and traffic conditions. A set of rules can start to look like the only thing that matters. The rules become a replacement for our internal values, instead of the add-on they are supposed to be.

So what does it mean, all this talk of ethical behaviour, doing the right thing and internal values? Where does it come from, this trustworthiness? The HSBC boss mentioned culture, and that is important. (If everyone else is doing it, surely it must be alright?) But it goes much deeper than that – back to the family. A study in Germany investigated people's attitudes to risk and trust. They found that, to a large extent, children had similar attitudes to one or both of their parents. That is, a risk-taking parent tends to have a risk-taking child; a trusting parent tends to have a trusting child. In many cases, both parents had similar attitudes to each other. So it looks like people choose partners with similar risk and trust attitudes, which reinforces the legacy to their children.

Why do we have similar attitudes to our parents? It could be genetic of course. However, the results of the German study suggest that our attitudes to risk and trust are not entirely due to our genes. We are apparently influenced by the way we are brought up. Is that such a surprise? And remember, it is more important how the parents behave than what they say!

TRUE LIES

Some truths should never be spoken,
Some sleeping dogs never woken.
Sometimes a lie
Is the truest reply.
Some rules are meant to be broken.

I Don't Believe It!

Trusting involves believing. Trust is about truth and to believe something is to accept that it is true. Imagine the following true scenario. The place was a remote sand dune known as Kill Devil Hill, near Kitty Hawk in North Carolina. The date was 17 December 1903. It was a great day for the brothers, Wilbur and Orville Wright. Their flying machine took to the air for the first time. It was off the ground for only 12 seconds but this was an important beginning. They made three more successful flights during the day, the longest one lasting almost a minute. However, as they were packing up at the end of the day, the flying machine was caught by a gust of wind and damaged beyond repair, never to fly again.

Orville Wright sent a telegram to their father, back home in Dayton Ohio, announcing their success and telling him to inform the press. As is so often the case, communicating the message turned out to be harder than they imagined. A few Dayton newspapers proudly wrote about the achievement of their local heroes. But the story that spread nationally was based on a leak from a telegraph operator. The few available facts were largely ignored. The story was cooked up into a fantastic tale that was so far fetched it made fun of the whole idea. In the end, most people simply did not believe the flights had taken place.

One person who read the early press reports and wanted to believe them was Amos Root. He was a wealthy businessman – a beekeeper – and an eccentric who loved new technology. By this time he was in his sixties and had left his beekeeping business in the care of his sons. He still kept control of the fortnightly magazine, *Gleanings in Bee Culture*. He wrote a regular column in his bee magazine about anything that interested him – a bit like a blog today. He had recently bought one of the new automobiles and he drove it the 175 miles to meet the Wright brothers in Dayton.

The brothers meanwhile were so focused on building a new flying machine that they neglected their bicycle-making business. They desperately needed to make some money from their flying but they were still struggling to get their designs patented. They avoided publicity. They didn't trust the press and were afraid of competition. Why it was that they trusted Amos Root is not clear. Perhaps it was because he shared their religious beliefs as well as their enthusiasm for engineering. Perhaps they saw him as a potential investor. Anyway, on 20 September 1904, the Wrights allowed Root to witness their first truly convincing demonstration. Their new flying machine took off, flew about a mile in a full circle and landed safely. Root was thrilled and wrote about it in his blog.

So it was that the birth of aviation came to be announced to the world in a beekeeping magazine.

Root also sent his report to *Scientific American*, but they refused to publish it. The scientific community did not believe in heavier-than-air flight.

SCIENTIFIC OPINION

Those two crazy brothers called Wright
Are said to have made the first flight.
A contraption that flies?
What a whole pack of lies!
We scientists know wrong from right.

O Ye of Little Faith

Over the years I have collected many books about risk. One of the first to make it onto my bookshelf was *Against the Gods* by Peter Bernstein. The first page of the introduction contains the following words:

> The revolutionary idea that defines the boundary between modern times and the past is the mastery of risk: the notion that the future is more than a whim of the gods and that men and women are not passive before nature.

The mastery of risk! What a bold claim – arrogant even. That was in 1996. Since then, there have been enough reports of industrial accidents, natural disasters and turmoil in the financial markets to convince most people that we humans are far from having achieved a mastery of risk.

Bernstein himself changed his view over the years. In 2006 he gave a lecture at the Institute of Chartered Financial Analysts in which he said this:

> If we stare at just the models and equations, we lose sight of the mystery of life – we lose sight of the unknown. There would be no such thing as risk if everything were known. If only a finite number of things could happen, risk would not exist. Even the most brilliant mathematical genius will never be able to tell us what the future holds. *What matters in thinking about risk is the quality of the decisions we make in the face of uncertainty.*

Quite a change! His thinking about risk has shifted from mastery to mystery. In the same lecture Bernstein even went on to speak about God and free will – in a presentation to financial analysts.

The front cover of *Against the Gods* is illustrated by a famous painting: *Storm on the Sea of Galilee* by Rembrandt. The painting depicts an incident described in *The Bible*. The fishermen in the boat are followers of Jesus of Nazareth. They are afraid that the storm will overwhelm the boat. They cry out to Jesus to save them. Jesus replies with the words, 'Why are ye fearful, O ye of little faith?' There it is: the essence of cool risk. The triumph of faith over fear. '*The Bible would* say that,' you might think, 'it's a religious book and faith is a religious word.' Yes, we do usually think of faith as something religious. The word 'faith' is sometimes even used to mean the same as 'religious' – like when we talk about 'faith schools'. However, when the word 'faith' was used in the first English translations of *The Bible*, it was not an especially religious word. Faith was simply about trusting.

The early English bibles had a huge impact on the development of the English language. The word 'faith' was not used in those days as a religious word. In fact it was the other way round. Faith is now thought of as something religious because it was used a lot in *The Bible*. The old, non-religious meaning still survives in other forms, such as 'faithful' and 'in good faith'. I would like to reclaim 'faith' back from the religions. Faith is a kind of trust that we all need. It overcomes fear and enables us to take worthwhile risks.

Faith and fear are opposite ends of a spectrum. At one end – the bad end – fear stifles risk taking. At the good end, faith reveals a vision of the possible. It is such a vision that encourages risk taking and opens up new opportunities. This spectrum from fear to faith is so important to the idea of cool risk that I like to give it a name: I call it the F-Spectrum.

I THINK, THEREFORE
I AM CONFUSED

They attempted, the thinkers of yore,
The meaning of life to explore.
Through most of our history
They thought it a mystery.
Today we are not quite so sure.

A Dog Called Fido

Faith, as it relates to the F-Spectrum, is not just about belief. The bee man, Root, believed the stories he heard about the Wright brothers' flying machine. The Wright brothers had a vision of the possible. That vision was nothing less than human flight. They needed more than belief to inspire them to take the necessary risks. Root had belief. The Wright brothers had faith. And we are not talking about 'blind' faith. This kind of faith is not blind. It is based on facts. In this case, the facts were these: the experience of the brothers, their engineering know-how and their determination. Their faith had a sound basis.

But of course, faith is more than just facts. Trust is a feeling we get about something or someone. It is an emotional response to the facts. It is something inside us. We call it 'confidence' from the Latin word '*fido*' meaning 'I trust'. Abraham Lincoln named his dog

Fido. He knew what it meant in Latin and it seemed a good name for his faithful friend.

Confidence enables us to take risks – in short, to *do* stuff. Part of the reason why people are less willing to take risks is that we expect to know everything. This makes us less well equipped to deal with uncertainty. We confuse being confident with being certain. However, confidence and certainty are different in an important way. Confidence requires trust, whereas certainty requires none. Certainty knows what will happen. Confidence does not know what to expect but trusts in the power to cope with any outcome. This power can be physical, psychological or spiritual.

In society today, trust tends to be seen as a weakness. A very trusting person is likely to be seen as gullible or a sucker. And yet trust is a normal part of being human. It is natural to feel good when acting in a trustworthy way. Remember oxytocin. It is unfortunate that, in our unreasonably reasonable world, trusting is seen as foolish, as weakness. It is unfortunate not least because trust is important for economic well-being. Research carried out by the economist Paul Zak (and others) measured levels of trust in more than 40 countries. This research showed that trust is low in poor countries and high in rich countries.

Human beings have evolved as essentially social animals. We function best not as individuals but as a community. It is trust that oils the wheels of society.

Hustlers and other thieves – and unscrupulous advertisers – abuse that trust for personal or corporate gain. These people are guilty of wrongdoing, just as much as those who exploit other natural feelings such as sex. Community – a sense of attachment – is necessary, not only for our economic well-being, but also for our physical and mental health.

How are we to instil a sense of trust and confidence in the citizens of tomorrow? Certainly not by protecting them from all risks. Confidence arises from learning and experience. Children need to be able to take risks so that they can develop into responsible, risk-taking adults. Of course they need to be protected from some things but they also need to learn how life works. And that means getting to grips with variety and uncertainty. It means taking risks.

LET THEM DO IT

Let them fall when they're learning to walk.
Let them laugh when they're learning to talk.
Let the girls really try.
Let the boys really cry.
Or else, life will come as a shock.

Faith, Hope and Chance

In October 1994 the United States launched Operation Gatekeeper, a new attempt to control illegal immigration along its 2000-mile, southern border. They erected new fences and increased the number of officers in the Border Patrol. The effect was to prevent migrants from using the easy crossing points. So the migrants turned their attention to more remote and dangerous places. Since the start of Operation Gatekeeper, thousands of migrants have died on this border. A few of them lost their lives being pursued by the Border Patrol. But most of them drowned in the Rio Grande or died of dehydration in the desert.

In 1995, the Schengen Agreement was implemented across a large part of Europe, allowing cross-border travel without passport checks. The main objective was to encourage closer co-operation between European states. However, this freedom has also encouraged would-be migrants from outside Europe, notably from Africa. They know that, if they can get into Italy or Greece in the south, then they can travel across Europe fairly easily. But getting into Europe is not easy. Once again, it is not so much the border patrols that present a risk, but the criminal gangs and the hazardous sea crossing from Africa.

Why do they do it? What drives so many thousands of Africans and South Americans to run the risk of a horrible death? There is the vision of a promised land. But that in itself is not enough. It is the situation at home that drives them to it. They are desperate. They are without hope. The prospects are bleak for them and their children. Hopelessness and despair drive people to take risks.

Faith and hope are often spoken of in the same breath. The impression is given that they mean much the same thing: a kind of wishful thinking, not much to do with reason. I have argued that faith is nothing of the sort. Faith – at least the kind of faith that inspires worthwhile risk taking – is a reasonable trust based on experience. Hope, on the other hand, *is* a kind of wishful thinking but still reasonable. It is more definite than faith. Hope is about things that can reasonably be expected to happen. Far from being similar to faith, hope – when it comes to risky behaviour – is almost the opposite. Risk taking is not encouraged by hope but by a lack of hope.

The word 'desperate' comes from Latin. It means 'without hope'. The Chambers 21st Century Dictionary defines 'desperate' as 'willing to take risks fearlessly because of hopelessness and despair'. Hopelessness? Despair? These sound like unhappiness! By sneaking up on it from behind, we almost have an answer to the question, 'How to be happy?' It can be summed up in three words: faith, hope and chance. Faith: confidence in yourself and others, based on experience. Hope: a reasonable expectation of something you want.

And chance? It is about being comfortable with uncertainty, closely bound up with faith and hope. Trusting allows us to be happy about uncertainty. It enables us to be content with not knowing everything. Trust helps us to face the future, which is always unknown.

SOME HOPE

'Hope springs eternal' – a quote
From *An Essay on Man* that Pope wrote.
In hundreds of lines
Of elaborate rhymes
There seem to be three words of note.

Chewing the Cud: Chapter Six

- Being trusted gives you a buzz.

- It is easy to lie, but more complex to tell the truth.

- What you do counts for more than what you say.

- Trust is not earned by following rules and avoiding risks.

- Cool risk is the triumph of faith over fear.

- Being confident is not the same as being certain.

- Trust allows us to be happy about uncertainty.

Cool Risk

CHAPTER SEVEN

GROWING

How investment banking works:

Everybody gives me all their money, and then everybody gets much more back.

No risk involved.

Cartoon by Michael Mittag

Escaping From Normal

Legg-Calvé-Perthes syndrome is a degenerative bone condition that damages the hip joint. It affects about 1 in 1000 children, mostly boys. Bill Shannon was one of the unlucky ones. He was using crutches by the time he was five years old. Over the years, he developed his own creative crutch technique that enabled him to get about more easily. According to him, he needed it to keep up with his little brother.

During his teenage years, Shannon was able to walk without crutches. He took up skateboarding and breakdancing – not the wisest choices, perhaps, for someone with his condition. By the time he was in his twenties, he was back on crutches. Sometimes he could walk only a few steps without them. Against all the odds, Shannon became an internationally acclaimed dancer and choreographer.

Although he made his name dancing with crutches, Shannon does not like to be thought of as a disabled dancer. He says, 'I'm an artist trapped in a human-interest story.' He is happier when he is accepted as an artist in his own right, such as when doing choreography for other dancers. Shannon's dancing blurs the boundary between 'disabled' and 'normal'. A dancer on crutches can do things that are impossible for other dancers. His work grew out of his experience using crutches as a child and his later breakdancing and skateboarding. He has always challenged the normal ways of seeing and doing.

Shannon has fired dancers for not being willing to take risks. However, the kinds of risk he had in mind were not physical ones. The dancers who didn't make the grade were not worried about a particularly dangerous move that might get them injured. No, what worried them was more likely to be a longer-than-usual, slow-motion section. It was artistic risks that Shannon was talking about, not physical risks. He needed his dancers to trust him – not just his skill as a performer but also his creative vision.

We enjoy stories like that of Bill Shannon – stories of triumph out of despair, a phoenix rising from the ashes, Saint George slaying the dragon. But, in a way, it is sad that we find stories like this so appealing. The fact that we find the story uplifting suggests that we have a dim view of normal. It means we have low expectations. We assign people a place in society and expect them to stay there. We cast people in a certain mould. Then we are surprised if they break out of it. We make it difficult for people to be different. Outstanding is out. Heroes are history.

NORMAL HEROISM

There once was knight we'll call G
Had a dragon to slay before tea.
Sometime after lunch
He developed a hunch
That the dragon was scareder than he.

Raising the Bar

The 1968 Summer Olympics were notable for several reasons. The location, Mexico City, was the highest altitude of any summer games. The Czechoslovakian gymnast, Věra Čáslavská, who won four gold medals, made a public protest against the recent Soviet invasion of Czechoslovakia. Two African-American sprinters on the medals podium raised their black-gloved fists in a civil-rights protest. However, the best cool risk story of the games was that of Dick Fosbury.

Fosbury competed in the high jump for the United States. He did not look much like an athlete and his jumping style was very different from that of the other competitors. He launched himself at the bar backwards at a peculiar angle – and landed in an ungainly heap on the other side. The media called it the Fosbury Flop and everyone enjoyed the joke. They only stopped laughing when Fosbury won the gold medal and set a new Olympic record. Fosbury had invented the new high jump. The old straddle style rapidly became extinct.

Just before being selected for the Olympic team, Fosbury had been thrown out of college. His engineering studies had suffered because he was spending too much time on his athletics training. America was at war in Vietnam. For Fosbury, being out of college meant he was supposed to go for military service. However, his army medical found damage to his spine from an old back injury. He was declared unfit for combat. He was free to go to Mexico City.

After his triumph at the Olympics, Fosbury went back to college. He qualified as a civil engineer and eventually started his own engineering company. He never really got back into international athletics, although he became active in the World Olympians Association, even serving as its President.

The stories of Bill Shannon and Dick Fosbury are not common risk stories, but they are about people taking risks. Taking risks brought about change in their own lives and touched the lives of many other people. It was not easy. They had to endure pain and ridicule. Both men had vision and determination that enabled them to act against the advice of others. Fosbury's coaches advised him to abandon his crazy jumping style, but he stuck with it. He not only won awards for himself. He changed the world of high jump forever. But it was not easy.

JUST DO IT

You just have to like it or lump it.
The trick is not yours till you trump it.
It's really bizarre
To keep raising the bar
Unless you are able to jump it.

Half a Glass

A well-known question: 'Is the glass half full or half empty?' The answer depends, of course, on who is answering:

The Optimist: 'The glass is half full.'

The Pessimist: 'The glass is half empty.'

The Engineer: 'The glass is twice as big as it needs to be.'

The Scientist: 'The glass is full – 51.3%
liquid and 48.7% air.'

The Psychologist: 'You're not going to catch
me with that one!'

The Down-and-Out: 'What glass?'

Optimist. Pessimist. We recognize these stereotypes. People *are* like that! The very existence of the words 'optimist' and 'pessimist' suggests a personal characteristic – not just temporary moods. The nature/nurture debate will never be fully resolved, but experience suggests that much of our individual make-up is what we are born with. It is up to us to make the best of it. Me? I tend to be pessimistic and sceptical, which doesn't sound promising. However, this personality helped me to be a successful project manager. Many projects fail because their managers are too hopeful and optimistic.

Whether optimist or pessimist, the important thing is to make the most of whatever you have. To do that you have to take risks – try new things. By doing this you can find out what you are good at. You also find out what you're not so good at, which can be painful at the time. In the long run, you can focus on your strengths and not worry about trying to be somebody you are not cut out to be.

The difficulty for those of us who are optimism-challenged is to bring ourselves to take these risks in the first place. But it is worth it. Such risk taking is how we discover our strengths and weaknesses. Optimists generally find it easier to take risks. Your typical pessimist, discouraged by one failure, ends up avoiding the next, all-important challenge. Discovering weakness is a scary prospect. Failure is a dirty word. But these are the teething troubles that give us teeth. In order to grow in the right direction we have to put out some shoots in the wrong direction.

What counts most is doing stuff. Many people are afraid of change. But change is what helps us to be happy. How do *you* see half a glass of your favourite drink? How you feel depends not so much on your personality but on whether you are pouring or drinking. Is the glass filling or emptying? The thing that has the biggest impact on how you feel is the way it is changing. As I showed with the checkerboard illusion in Chapter Four, we are more sensitive to differences than absolute values. It is easier to feel happy when things are improving.

DISTURBING THE PEACE

If you don't like your order deranged
Or the things on your desk rearranged
Then what you should know
If you're going to grow
Is that something is bound to be changed.

A Tall Tale

The United States used to be the tallest nation in the world. Not any more. Over the last 150 years, Europe has grown. The average height in Europe used to be way below what it was in America. Now it is significantly greater. The Dutch and the Scandinavians are the tallest, but the Germans and even the Brits are not far behind them. Americans, on the other hand, have hardly grown for over 50 years. The Dutch have achieved the most impressive rise. In 100 years they have gone from being the smallest in Europe to the tallest of the tall.

How did they do it? Think about a typical Dutchman. Let's call him Wim. There is nothing he can do to change his height – or *lengte* as the Dutch call it. (The way the Dutch talk about their length, rather than their height, makes me think of them as lying down rather than standing up.) Wim is grown up. Say his height is a bit above average: 48% of Dutchmen are taller than Wim and 52% shorter than him. His height fits at a certain place in the spectrum of Dutch male heights. The spectrum stretches from the very short (for the Dutch, anyway) all the way up to the very tall (even for the Dutch). Wim knows his place in the spectrum. He cannot make himself taller or shorter.

The Dutch got taller by shifting the whole spectrum upwards. There are still Dutchmen who are on the short side and others who are on the tall side. But the short ones are taller than they would have been a century ago. The tall ones are pushing new boundaries. Doorways are being raised and public transport redesigned. Our friend Wim can do nothing about his own height, but he can take care of the health and nutrition of his children. When good healthcare and education are available to most of the population, then that population grows up.

This spectrum shift has been most remarkable in Holland but it has happened to some extent all over Europe. There is still some debate about the factors that can shift the height spectrum but some things are clear. The height of a nation is closely related to its general health and prosperity. We do all our growing in childhood. So things that affect children have the biggest effect on height. Therefore, care for women and their babies at birth is important. Diet is a key factor. But there are other things that have less direct impact on height, which also seem to be important. One of these is the sharing of wealth. Nations with an extreme spread of wealth – those with a big gap between the rich and the poor – tend to be shorter.

One thing to note about changing the height of a nation is that it is a slow process. Shifting the spectrum cannot happen overnight. The change comes about by caring for children. The youngsters then grow up to be taller than the previous generation. Therefore, the increase in height of the population only becomes really noticeable when these healthier children grow up. An individual like Wim might not even see the change in his own family. His children might not be taller than him. But, on average, in a healthy society, the people grow taller.

In the last few years, the Dutch have stopped growing. We don't know yet whether this is because they have reached the maximum allowed by their genes. Or perhaps Dutch life is getting less healthy. Time will tell.

LENGTH RESTRICTION

There once was a Dutchman called Wim
Who spent every day at the gym
But try as he might
At increasing his height
His kids remained taller than him.

I'll Drink To That!

Alcohol has been part of the story of mankind for many thousands of years. Generally speaking, people like to drink it. They like the effect it has. After drinking small amounts, people feel happier. Social interaction becomes easier. Unfortunately, alcohol is not good for you. It is toxic and addictive. It is terribly easy to drink too much. Depending on how alcohol affects you personally, it can lead to aggression or depression. Alcohol contributes to large amounts of illness and crime, especially violent crime. In a word, alcohol is a problem.

What has this got to do with cool risk? I am not recommending alcohol. Although drinking small quantities of alcohol can have social benefits, larger amounts - surprisingly moderate amounts - can have major drawbacks. The main reason for mentioning alcohol here is that it is a good example of spectrum shift. The subject has been studied for a long time and there is good research evidence.

Figure 3 shows the spectrum of alcohol intake for a certain population. In the middle, a large number of people drink a moderate amount of alcohol. On the right, small numbers of people drink very little. Teetotallers are at the extreme right. On the left, a small number of people drink to excess; that's where the alcoholics are. The shaded area at the left represents people who have a drink problem. It is not easy to define exactly what we mean by a drink problem. But suppose that the vertical line in the diagram represents the 'problem threshold'. Anything to the left of this line is a problem. The total number of people with a drink problem is shown by the size of the shaded area.

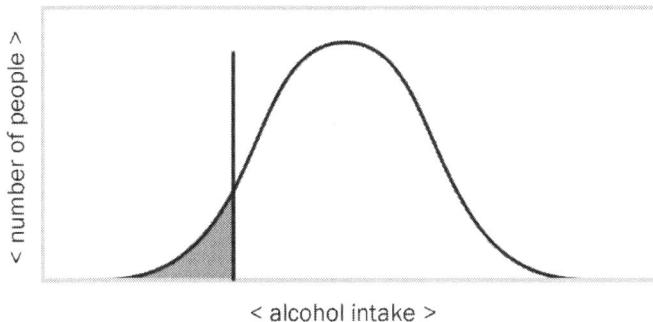

< alcohol intake >

Figure 3

One way of tackling the alcohol problem is to focus on the problem drinkers – to try to help them drink less. In terms of Figure 3, this means dragging people out of the shaded area and pushing them further up the slope. However, researchers have found that this approach has limited success. The people who have just struggled out of the shaded area often fall back down again. And, even when some people manage to escape from the problem zone, there are always others just above it who fall down to replace them.

The research shows that a more effective way of tackling the problem is to shift the whole spectrum, as illustrated in Figure 4. In this case, the general intake of alcohol is reduced – that is, shifted to the right. The shaded area becomes smaller, which means the number of problem drinkers is reduced. This approach is also not easy. It involves persuading people to drink less even when they themselves do not have a drink problem. But this is easier than helping an addict to cut down.

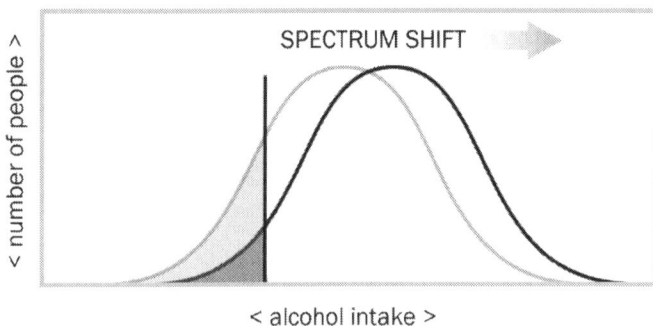

Figure 4

The example is necessarily simplified. The shape of the spectrum is not really symmetrical as it is in the diagrams. Also, when there is a spectrum shift, there will also be some change in the shape of the spectrum. The researchers found that the spectrum shift did not significantly change the number of teetotallers. People who go without alcohol completely do so for a variety of reasons that are not related to the general level of drinking in their society. They may be recovering alcoholics or they may have religious reasons. Or they may have personalities that put a low value on the social benefits of alcohol.

SOCIAL DRINKING

I am not alcoholic as such
But perhaps I am drinking too much
So I'll try to reform –
To drink less than the norm –
Try shifting the spectrum a touch.

Well, Well, Well

The ancient Romans loved bath time. Even at the furthest reaches of the empire, wealthy Romans had to have their baths. They developed technology to provide hot baths. They also sought out places with natural hot springs. In Britain, one such place was already known to the local Celtic people. The Romans built a major bath and temple complex there, dedicated to the Celtic goddess, Sulis. Eventually this became the modern city of Bath. The town of Spa, in modern Belgium, was also a Roman bath town. The name of the Belgian town gave us the English word 'spa'.

Towns all over Europe grew up around springs of supposedly healing water. They usually included some reference to the water in their names, just to make sure everybody knew about their special status. Bath and Spa have only the water for a name! Other famous spa towns are Tunbridge Wells and Leamington Spa in England, Aix-les-Bains in France, Bad Homburg in Germany and Leukerbad in Switzerland. The German for bath is '*Bad*' which doesn't sound good in English. So, the German-speaking spa industry has adopted an English word: 'wellness'.

Wellness, of course, means simply the opposite of illness. The word has been part of the language for centuries. But, during the last century, it became much more popular – fashionable even. 'Wellness' means much the same as 'health'. However, the health industry had become too focussed on illness, instead of wellness. Health care was all about diseases, about surgery and giving people drugs to interfere with the natural processes in the body. When people started to concentrate on real health – which actually means wholeness – they looked for a different word. They turned to wellness.

Wellness takes a positive attitude to health, as opposed to a negative obsession with illness and disease. Wellness – in the sense of wellbeing – even reaches beyond health into every aspect of life. To be well is not just to be free from illness. It is also to grow, to flourish, to prosper. It is all too easy to think of economic growth, at the expense of other kinds of growth. When we talk today about somebody being 'prosperous' we usually mean they are wealthy. However, it has meant more than this for ages. In Shakespeare's *Romeo and Juliet*, it is Romeo who speaks the line, 'Live and be prosperous'. *Star Trek* picked this up in the Vulcan saying, 'Live long and prosper'. In both these uses, prosperous does not mean wealthy. It means something like successful, fortunate or flourishing – rather like happy, in fact.

The Legatum Prosperity Index™ is a report that is published every year. The report studies the wealth and wellbeing of people in most countries. The statistics in the report apply to more than 90% of the world population. The prosperity analysis covers not only economics but also health, freedom, government, safety, education, opportunity and community spirit. The thing in the report that attracts most media attention is a league table of countries, ranked in order of prosperity. The list is remarkably similar to the list of countries ranked in order of physical height.

Wellness is a great idea. It embraces a positive attitude to life. It is all inclusive. However, the idea of wellness has been hijacked. It became too fashionable. It should have been about opportunities for everyone. But it has been taken over by the rich. The wellness industry of today is just like the spas of yesterday and the Roman baths of history. Wellness has become a forum for the rich and powerful. Admittedly, the five-star hotels offering 'wellness weekends' do have *something* to do with health and fitness. But they are usually attempting to combat the side effects of affluence – things like heart disease, diabetes and obesity. They are not actually trying to increase the wellbeing of society.

NOT SO WELL

There once was a couple of friends
Who were mad about wellness weekends.
But their aim was not health –
More like flaunting their wealth
And following fashions and trends.

Get Happy . . .

Optimism, happiness and cool risk go together. Optimists tend to be happier and more willing to take risks. To some extent, these characteristics are just part of your personality. They are fixed by your genes. But only to some extent. You might be an optimist, a happy person, a risk taker. Or maybe you are a pessimist, prone to depression and worried about risk. Most likely you are somewhere in between the two extremes. You are at a certain place in the spectrum. This place is controlled by your genes. People talk about a happiness thermostat or a risk thermostat. You can move up and down the spectrum a little bit but, after a while, you settle back to the same old place.

Genes are not everything, though. Human height is definitely controlled by genes. But it is also affected by poverty, disease and inequality. Increased height can be achieved by spectrum shift. A healthy society grows taller. It is similar with happiness. While, in principle, your genes define your happiness profile, this does assume a certain level of health. And when it comes to happiness, it is mental health that is more important than physical health. A society with a higher level of mental health is happier.

What I said about alcohol intake also applies to mental health. Have a look at Figure 5. This is like Figure 4 – except that now the horizontal line represents happiness. In Figure 5, the right-hand side of the picture represents people who are supremely happy. I won't bother about them; they can look after themselves! The shaded area on the left represents people who have a level of unhappiness that is classed as mental illness, such as depression or anxiety. Just like with alcohol problems, it is hard to move people permanently up the curve, out of the darkness that is mental illness.

In modern medical studies, there is an increasing focus on wellness. This does not mean the expensive spa treatments called wellness. The modern focus is on wellness as the opposite of illness. In the case of mental health, this means thinking about the majority of us, who are not classed as mentally ill. If we can shift the happiness spectrum upwards, it will have many benefits. First of all, we can simply enjoy more feelings of happiness!

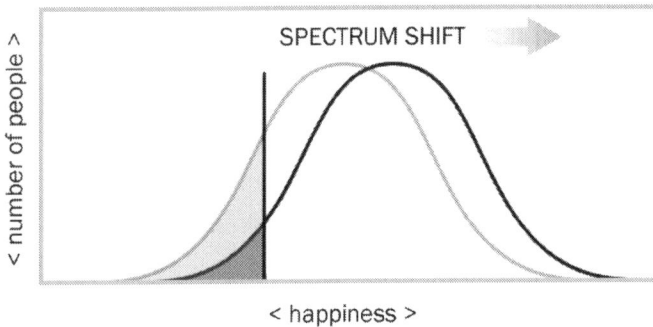

Figure 5

As the happiness spectrum shifts to the right, the shaded area on the left gets smaller. This means a smaller number of people with mental illness. Not only is this good news for those who are happiness-challenged. It is good for the whole society because it reduces the problems and expense caused by mental illness.

So how do we do it? How to shift the happiness spectrum?

WELL HAPPY

Happiness, sometimes we find,
Is with physical health intertwined
But plenty of witness
Puts physical fitness
Below someone's wellness of mind.

. . . Start Early

It is a funny thing: most of us would like more happiness and yet many of us are afraid of change. We want to be happier but we don't want to change. And yet, to find more happiness, something has to change. Not all change is for the better, though, so change involves risk. Unless we risk something, we can never make the changes we want. Therefore, in order to become happier, we need to take some risks. Becoming happier is not exactly like growing taller, but any change for the better is a kind of growth.

There is a limit to what you can achieve on your own. If you focus on your own happiness, you don't get a lot happier. That's the trouble with a lot of self-help books; they try to help your self. At the end of the day, they are too selfish – and selfishness does not lead to happiness. Strange as it may seem, helping other people leads to more happiness. Community spirit does more for overall happiness than individual attempts to get happy. In the end, a happy society leads to happy individuals.

It does not happen overnight. Spectrum shift is a slow process. There are things we can do as individuals. We can smile at people. We can be trustworthy and be ready to trust others. These go some way to spreading happiness. But real growth in happiness comes about in the community. Caring for children is an important part of it. This does not mean giving children everything they want – far from it! It means providing good health and education. It means giving children a balanced attitude to risk. It means showing them how to trust and to be trusted. The key word here is 'showing'. It is not enough just to tell them. Remember that people – especially children – learn more from how we behave than what we say.

A few years ago, I was attending a conference in southern Uganda. Most of the participants were Africans – development workers from all over Uganda and from neighbouring countries. They had come together to share experiences and learn from each other, as well as to hear from some external advisors. On the first evening, there was an informal gathering, where people were invited to share their life stories. What impressed me most about these personal histories were the dramatic accounts of getting an education. Parents had made heroic sacrifices to enable their children to be educated. Children had walked 10km to get to school – and another 10km to get home at the end of the day. I listened in the semi-darkness to these personal stories and struggled to hold back tears. These were people who were making a difference in their communities. And their ability to make a difference was largely thanks to their amazing opportunities for education as children.

If we want to grow as a community, we have to act as a community. If we want to grow taller, healthier and happier, we have to help each other on the way. It is only as a community that we can develop a cool attitude to risk – to trust and to be trusted. Nobody can trust on their own. Above all, these changes are most dramatic when we focus on the young. If we help children to grow taller, healthier and happier, we benefit them and the future society. And we feel good ourselves into the bargain.

RISKING HAPPINESS

You can give an unwarranted gift.
You can offer a stranger a lift.
Yes, it's risky for sure
But it helps to ensure
That the happiness spectrum will shift.

Chewing the Cud: Chapter Seven

- Break out of the mould.

- Change is not easy, but it is worth trying.

- What counts most is doing stuff.

- Spectrum shift: to really make a difference.

- Spectrum shift is not easy.

- But it's easier than individual struggle.

- Spread a little happiness.

- Teach children to risk and trust.

CHAPTER EIGHT

LETTING GO

Cartoon by Michael Mittag

A Bird in the Hand

This last chapter is about letting go. It begins, like many stories, in a pub. But the pub is not just any old pub. It is an ancient country inn, in the English County of Berkshire. Its most famous guest was King George III, first king of the United Kingdom. Other lords and ladies may have stayed there too, on their way between London and the fashionable spa at Bath. The inn is said to be over 600 years old – and haunted. But the most interesting thing about the inn from my point of view is its name. It is called the 'Bird in Hand'.

The origin of the name is lost in the mists of time but I believe it comes from the old proverb, 'A bird in the hand is worth two in the bush'. The proverb is certainly old. It was known in the Middle Ages. Variants of this proverb even date back to Roman times. There are many pubs in Britain named the 'Bird in Hand' or something similar. The town of Newhey in Yorkshire has two, both in the same street. One is the 'Bird in Hand' while the other is the 'Bird in the Hand'. The locals call them the 'Top Bird' and 'Bottom Bird' to tell them apart.

In the United States, there is a village called Bird-in-Hand in Lancaster County, Pennsylvania. The village community was founded in the early 1700s just before King George III was born. The Bird-in-Hand village inn apparently bore a sign depicting not only a bird in a hand but also a bush with another two birds!

The proverb is about risk taking. It is about letting go. It is connected with the loss aversion I mentioned in Chapter Three. Remember Daniel Kahneman? He was the psychologist who walked away with the Nobel Prize in economics for his work on Prospect Theory. Kahneman's ground-breaking studies were the first to measure people's reluctance to let go. He wondered how much he needed to offer people in order to persuade them to give up what they had already. He devised some studies and worked it all out. In the end, he calculated that the ratio was 2 to 1, just like the proverb says: two in the bush to one in the hand.

The bird-in-hand proverb describes a very basic human trait – reluctance to let go of what we have. Some people have suggested other origins for the proverb. One popular explanation relates to the practice of hunting with birds of prey, such as falcons. The bird in the hand would be the falcon and the birds in the bush would be the prey. However, the numbers don't fit if that were the case. The bird in the hand would be far more valuable than two in the bush. So the ratio of 2 to 1 does not make sense with this explanation.

The way the proverb is used today emphasizes the loss aversion aspect of risk taking. People use the proverb when they want to stick with what they have. They are thinking, 'Better not risk it'. I have never heard it used to support going after the two birds in the bush!

Upsetting the Proverbials

Cancel whatever is planned!
Never mind if you don't understand.
When shove comes to push
Then two birds in the bush
Are worth risking one in the hand.

The Goodbye Kiss

Imagine the scene. It is a busy airport. A young woman is about to take a flight. She is already in the passengers-only departure area. While the security officer is distracted, a young man slips through security. He ignores the risks. He has one single-minded purpose: to kiss his lover one last time. It sounds like the closing moments of a Hollywood romance. We see the couple locked in a passionate embrace as the tears and the credits roll.

But this is not Hollywood fiction. It really happened – at New York's Newark Airport on 3 January 2010. A member of the public saw the young man slip through security unchallenged and alerted airport staff. Very quickly, a full scale security alert was in operation. The airport was shut down for several hours. Thousands of people had their travel disrupted. Many of them had to wait in line to pass through security checks for a second time.

A goodbye kiss. So simple and innocent. And yet so powerful. We find it hard to let go – to say goodbye. We always want to keep hold of our bird in the hand. The kiss speaks of an emotional attachment. It is this that makes it hard to say goodbye. The airport story is an extreme example but letting go is always emotional. We sometimes speak about 'being emotional' as if it is a bad thing. But emotions are involved in almost all decision making. Of course, it doesn't do to let emotions get out of hand, but we have to accept that emotions often play a significant part. To put it bluntly, we must expect to suffer.

Don't get me wrong. I am not recommending suffering for its own sake. Suffering is only good as a path to a worthwhile outcome. This is the principle of sacrifice. It started out as a religious thing. The word 'sacrifice' literally means 'to do something holy'. In ancient times, a sacrifice involved giving up something – letting go of something – such as a prized animal. This is important. It had to be one of the best animals, not some weak diseased creature that would be easy to give up. The purpose of the sacrifice was to please a god, perhaps in expectation of some community benefit such as a good harvest.

The principle of sacrifice is still relevant today. We don't need to be killing animals – or even believe in a god. We might not think of it as doing something holy but we can accept sacrifice as doing something worthwhile – heroic even. Sacrifice involves kissing goodbye to something you love in order to achieve a greater good. It might mean travelling less, or eating less meat, for the sake of the environment. It could mean refusing a cream cake, or saying no to a cigarette, for a healthier life. It might mean kissing goodbye to someone you love, to allow them the freedom to live their own life. It could even mean risking your life to save someone else.

Sacrifice is a natural part of most worthwhile risk taking – letting go of something you love in the hope of a greater good. Yes, sacrifice does involve suffering. Not suffering for its own sake, but suffering none the less. We tend to think of loss or pain as suffering. But this is to confuse suffering with the cause of the suffering. Loss or pain is not the same thing as suffering. How do you feel about the pain? That is the suffering! It's difficult to separate how you feel about it – which is the real suffering – from the stuff that caused it.

The Ancient Greek word for 'suffering' was 'pathos', which is the root of the English word 'passion'. Originally it concentrated on the bad stuff that happened, like in the title of the movie, *The Passion of the Christ*. Today, 'passion' usually focuses more on the emotional side. In the airport anecdote, I used the expression 'a passionate embrace'. It describes an emotional intensity in the kiss more than the loss of parting.

VIRTUAL REALITY

You experience pleasure and pain.
You encounter a loss or a gain.
These things may be real,
But the way that you feel
Is what happens inside of your brain.

Just Not Fair

The British Equality and Human Rights Commission was created in 2007. It was required by law to report to Parliament every three years. Their first report, in 2010, was titled *How fair is Britain?* It took them 750 pages to answer this question. The word 'risk' appears in those pages almost as many times as the word 'fair'. So it seems clear that the two concepts are closely related – at least in the minds of the report's authors. I confess I have not read all 750 pages but here is an extract from the Executive Summary:

> Britain is a country increasingly at ease with its diversity, proud of its heritage of 'fair play' and supportive of the ideals of equality and human rights . . . However, the evidence shows clearly that whatever progress has been made for some groups in some places, the outcomes for many people are not shifting as far or as fast as they should.

So the answer to the question 'How fair is Britain?' seems to be: good in theory but not so good in practice. Not exactly a gold star for the nation that invented fairness. The concept of fair play is so fundamentally British that it is exported to other languages without translation: *le fair-play* in French and *das Fairplay* in German. Even in the English document quoted above, 'fair play' is surrounded by quotation marks, suggesting it is something special.

But what is fairness? The principle of fairness is summarized in the phrase, 'Do as you would be done by'. It is a principle of give and take that allows a group to function. The group might be the citizens of a nation or the players in a game. But, whatever the group, there has to be an understanding that, in order for the group to function, members will not act selfishly. The group members agree to a set of rules (or laws). The rules are enforced to ensure that fairness prevails. However, in most societies, the rules are made by the most powerful members of the group. So the society is more or less unfair. The concept of fairness in one culture can be very different from what it is in another culture. But the principle of fairness is the same: members of the group have to moderate their individual aspirations for the good of the group. They have to let something go.

Justice depends on fairness but the two things are not the same. Justice is usually judged against the rules and not against any basic principle of fairness. Fair play is indeed something special. People sometimes define it as 'playing within the rules' but I think this misses the point altogether. Fair play is more than keeping to the rules. It is ethical behaviour that is not covered by the rules, or perhaps even breaks the rules. When a soccer referee penalizes a player for committing a foul, that's justice. If a player kicks the ball out of play because an injured opponent needs attention, that's fair play.

REVENGE

True justice is something pristine.
Conversely, revenge is obscene.
While justice is fair,
Helping people to share,
Revenge is just selfish and mean.

Taking a Guilt Trip

The headquarters of Swiss International Air Lines is in France. This anomaly comes about because, although the city of Basel is in Switzerland, its airport is some 4km over the border in France. Access to the airport from Basel is via a Swiss road on French soil. The fences on either side of the road are effectively the border between France and Switzerland. Passengers landing at Basel have to make sure they take the correct exit from the terminal building to avoid ending up in France instead of Switzerland.

Once outside the terminal on the Swiss side, you can take a bus into the city. There are machines where you can buy a ticket, using either Swiss Francs or Euros. Lots of people get on the bus without buying a ticket because many Basel residents have a season ticket. There is a sign inside the bus that proclaims in large letters, '*Schwarzfahren ist unfair*' (riding without paying is unfair). In smaller letters, it details the fines payable for Schwarzfahring. But nobody seems to check. I have travelled this route dozens of times and I have never once seen a ticket inspector. The Swiss have a strong sense of fairness and public duty – and they clearly expect their visitors to have similar standards.

I must have made hundreds of trips on the Basel bus and tram network. In all those trips, I have had my ticket checked fewer than ten times. I have always travelled with a valid ticket. That's partly because my own personal sense of fairness rivals even the most fastidious Swiss. I would simply be unable to bear the guilty feeling of riding without a ticket. It is this feeling that encourages fairness, even in the absence of written rules. If a friend invites me to dinner a couple of times, and I have not offered him dinner in return, I feel guilty. I continue to feel guilty until I have re-established our friendship on a more equal basis by inviting him to dinner.

Guilt is a tricky thing. It comes in two flavours: one is factual, the other emotional. The first flavour is the kind you find in a court of law – guilty or not guilty. It concentrates on the facts. You either broke the law or you did not. It should not matter what anyone feels about it. The second flavour is the one with the bitter taste. This is the guilty feeling – the feeling of shame. It can be a good thing. If you did something unfair, it is right that you should feel guilty. The guilt already starts working while you are still *thinking about* doing wrong.

The problem with guilt as a feeling is that it can get out of proportion. A small misdemeanour can give rise to a whole sack-load of guilt. You can even feel guilty when you have done nothing wrong at all. This is when it is time to let go. Time to recognise that things have got out of hand. A little reflection might show that you are blaming yourself for something that is not your fault. So let it go. On the other hand, if you decide that you *are* guilty of causing some sort of unfairness then do something about it!

CHAMPIONS OF FAIRNESS

The British invented fair play.
You used to be able to say
That they shared an awareness
Of communal fairness.
The Swiss are the champions today.

No Undo

For many years, the majority of South Africans were forced to endure a regime based on racial segregation. In 1948, the segregation was formalized into a system called *apartheid*. Over the years, many atrocities were carried out by the white minority in the name of *apartheid*. Atrocities were also committed by some of the rebels who were trying to overthrow the regime. By the time the system was finally brought to an end in 1993, there was a lot of bad feeling on both sides.

The South African President, F.W. de Klerk, released Nelson Mandela from jail. Mandela was President of the African National Congress. He had spent 27 years in prison for his anti-*apartheid* activities. Both men knew that it was a time to move on and not a time for bitter recriminations. They negotiated an Interim Constitution, which recognized all South Africans as equal. The new constitution contained these words:

The adoption of this Constitution lays the secure foundation for the people of South Africa to transcend the divisions and strife of the past, which generated gross violations of human rights, the transgression of humanitarian principles in violent conflicts and a legacy of hatred, fear, guilt and revenge. These can now be addressed on the basis that there is a need for understanding but not for vengeance, a need for reparation but not for retaliation, a need for ubuntu but not for victimisation.

Based on the vision expressed in the Constitution, Mandela set up the Truth and Reconciliation Commission. This body helped to achieve a fairly orderly transition to the new South Africa. The process had many flaws but it was probably the least bad option. It has been the model for many other post-conflict situations since. The Commission was chaired by Desmond Tutu, who was Archbishop of Cape Town at the time. Tutu later wrote about his experience on the Commission in a book called *No Future without Forgiveness*. There it is, another F word: forgiveness.

Tutu was a Christian cleric. So you might expect him to be in favour of forgiveness. After all, forgiveness was an important part of the message of Jesus of Nazareth. (Sadly, this bit of the message is often ignored by people who call themselves Christians.) However, the idea of forgiveness does not need to be religious. Forgiveness is a valuable strategy for any human being. An internet search quickly turns up several websites that promote forgiveness:

- The Forgiveness Project
  (www.theforgivenessproject.com)

- The Forgiveness Web
  (www.forgivenessweb.com)

- Campaign for Forgiveness Research
  (www.forgiving.org).

All these examples claim to be non-religious.

To forgive is to accept that life has no undo button. There is no going back. Forgiveness is a decision to leave the past to itself and to embrace the future. Forgiveness means letting go. The word itself means to give away completely. Forgiveness does not deny wrongdoing. In fact, there can be no forgiveness if there was no wrong done. Some people shy away from forgiveness because they don't want to let the offender 'get away with it'. But forgiving does not mean letting the offender go free from punishment or reparation. When forgiveness is working well, the greatest benefit is for the victim, not for the offender.

Forgiveness is not easy. It involves risk. Many of the victims who testified to the Truth and Reconciliation Commission in South Africa found themselves unable to forgive. Forgiveness sometimes requires a heroic effort. But the benefits are worth the heroic effort. There is plenty of evidence that being able to forgive is associated with improved mental health.

Improved mental health means greater happiness. One of the studies that found a link between forgiveness and improved mental health was carried out in South Africa. Victims of atrocities who had not testified to the Commission were able to benefit from forgiveness just as much as those who had. It was not their testimony that was important but the personal decision to let it go.

GIVING IT AWAY

Forgiveness is hard to bestow.
It has big advantages, though.
And the good it engenders
Is not for offenders,
But victims prepared to let go.

The Fear of Missing Out

The Black Swan by Nassim Taleb is a bestselling book about highly improbable events. Basically, it is a book about risk so I had to read it. And I did actually finish it, although I found the author's style arrogant and annoying. The book contains a lot of personal anecdotes. The one I liked best is in the last, short chapter. (Or perhaps that's the only one I can remember!) Taleb tells the story of when he was studying in Paris and a fellow student stopped him from running to catch a train on the *Métro*. I particularly like his summary: 'Missing a train is only painful if you run after it'.

It's all in the mind. What makes it painful or not is how you feel about it. Of course, it makes a difference which train you miss. On the Paris *Métro*, another train will probably be along in a few minutes. So it's fairly easy to be cool about missing one. Not quite so easy to stay cool if you miss the last train that would have got you to the airport in time for your flight. Or perhaps missing a flight is not such a big deal either.

You can be happy only in the present – the here and now. But feelings about the present are coloured by remembering the past and contemplating the future. Staying cool about whether you catch a train or not comes from being able to accept an alternative future. Think about it. Suppose the future is not what you expect. Things could turn out worse than you hoped – or they might be better. Multiple alternative futures are possible. It depends on many things, only one of which is how you decide to act now. If you are ready to make the best of whatever future opens up for you, it gives you space and time to enjoy the present.

Being happy in the present does not mean wishing the present moment could last forever. Happiness now will almost certainly include good feelings about the future. But the trick seems to be this: to be happy about the variety of interesting and uncertain future opportunities. It is good to have a number of options to explore. But not so that you can decide which one you want. Fixing on one future possibility as the only desirable outcome leaves you open to anxiety, frustration and disappointment.

Being open to alternative futures is not the same as desiring them all. While you are ready to embrace whatever future opens up, you need to be prepared to let go of the options that remain behind closed doors. Otherwise you can be troubled by the fear of missing out. You might worry that, whichever course of action you choose, you could be missing out on something better. The expression 'to miss out' on something is relatively new – less than a hundred years old. It means to end up not having something that you were expecting, or had a right to. It seems to be a modern idea that goes along with the attitude that we should be able to know everything and have anything we want.

The fear of missing out has become so much part of popular culture that it has its own slang word: FOMO. Alright, it's more of an abbreviation than a word, since it is still usually written in capital letters. FOMO is a kind of insecurity. You want to have your cake and eat it. FOMO is worry about making the wrong decisions, taking the wrong risks. It is a kind of unhappiness.

I Diddums My Way

I hate it when things go astray.

I want things to happen my way.

I'm allergic to waiting

And find it frustrating

If diddums can't have it today.

Non, Je Ne Regrette Rien

When my children were small, I took a job in Scotland. And so it happened that my children started school there. One of the songs they learned in the kindergarten was 'Three Craws Sat Upon A Wall'. In the song, it is cold and frosty and the crows are all suffering for one reason or another:

- The first craw fell and broke his jaw.

- The second craw couldnae flee at a'. [couldn't fly at all]

- The third craw was greetin' for his ma'. [crying for his mum]

- The fourth craw wasnae there at a'.

The kids loved it. We all loved it! Because the lyrics are funny and sung to such a jolly tune, it feels like a happy song. How could we enjoy singing about such unfortunate crows? Why would we teach our children to be so heartless?

The fact is: it is not heartless to be happy after misfortune. It is healthy. Happiness now is reduced if we let the past bother us. Bad things do happen, of course. When they do, grief is normal. But then we have to let go. Dwelling on the past – thinking how things might have turned out differently – leads to unhappiness. The word 'regret' means literally to 'weep about the past'. It is related to the dialect word 'greet', meaning to cry, which is still used in Scotland and the north of England. That's what the third crow was doing in the song.

Regret tends to be personal. It is not a generalized weeping about history. If I feel regret, it is because of something I did. Regret wonders how things might have been had I acted some other way. In this respect, regret is like FOMO; it is linked to the decisions I make myself. The difference is that regret is about the past, whereas the fear of missing out – or any other type of anxiety – has more to do with the future.

Almost every decision involves uncertainty and, therefore, risk. If there is no doubt about the right choice it is hardly a decision at all – sometimes called a no-brainer. Once you make a decision, it requires commitment if you are going to be happy about it. Commitment and happiness? This might sound strange to a world that regards commitment as something undesirable. Commitment – to many people – sounds like an obligation, a burden, a restriction. These things don't seem like the ingredients of a cake you would want to have and eat.

Many dictionaries give several meanings for the word 'decide'. One of the meanings they usually give is 'to make something certain'. But this is not what deciding is really about. A decision does not make a risk less risky. In most cases, the uncertainty is still there after a decision is made. What would have happened if I had made a different decision? No, the word 'decide' means to 'cut off'. To decide means to reject the alternatives. Commitment is accepting the decision and letting go of the alternatives. Commitment is accepting that the future starts now – not from some wistfully-remembered moment in the past. No regrets.

CUTTING OFF A PIECE OF CAKE

The choice is not easy to make.
The decision is no piece of cake.
Yes, I've got to admit
There's a need to commit –
But what if I make a mistake?

A Life to Die For

What do philosophers do? They think about the meaning of life. Havi Carel is a philosopher. Her first book was a scholarly work called *Life and Death in Freud and Heidegger*. The book explores how death affects the way we think about life. One month after publication of her book, Carel was diagnosed with a lung condition known as LAM (lymphangioleiomyomatosis). It is extremely rare and there is no cure. Carel searched online and Wikipedia told her she had a life expectancy of about 10 years. She was stunned and asked the familiar question: 'Why me?'

After some months, her training and experience as a philosopher were able to help her through her ordeal – although she still found the practical harder than the theory. Philosophy is the search for wisdom but it is no good being wise for its own sake. Wisdom should help us to be happy. Carel realized that part of this wisdom is to recognise that we cannot change the past and have little control over the future. The present is the only place we can enjoy happiness. She recalled the words of Goethe who talked of 'the exquisite feel of the present'.

We often ask – why? It is tempting to think that, because we understand so much these days, we should know everything. The great scientist, Lord Kelvin, is famous for saying, 'There is nothing new to be discovered in physics now'. That was in 1900. He was, of course, spectacularly wrong. The question

'Why?' is an essential part of the human quest for knowledge, for the meaning of life and death. But all of us - including philosophers, scientists and theologians - must also be able to say 'Wow!' We need to be able to stand back in amazement. To accept that we do not know. To just wonder.

Knowledge is a bit like wealth. Up to a point, it is a good thing, especially when it is shared. However, it is unhealthy - yes, unhappy - to expect to know everything. So let's be relaxed about not knowing everything. Sometimes it is better to marvel, to wonder - to think 'Wow!' instead of 'Why?' Happiness comes more from accepting uncertainty and less from trying to explain the past and control the future.

Another philosopher who has something to say about death is Timothy Chappell. As well as being a professor of philosophy, he is also a mountaineer. So when he speaks about risk, I'm ready to listen. After a serious fall on Ben Nevis in 2008, Chappell wrote about the fear of death. At the time of his fall, he was sure he was going to die. But he was not afraid. He said he was more frightened afterwards in hospital, when he was about to have a general anaesthetic. He decided that his anxiety about being put to sleep was fear of losing control.

We know we can never have complete control over everything. But often that does not stop us trying to achieve it. In reality, an ability to relinquish control - to let go - can bring peace and happiness. This is what most of the world's religions are seeking at heart. They urge people to give up what they do not need. The word Islam means 'surrender' in Arabic. Letting go involves risk. It means stepping into the unknown. But rather than fearing an uncertain future, it is better to look forward to an enjoyable new present.

FROM WHY TO WOW

Happiness no one can buy.
However, a little less 'Why?'
And a little more 'Wow!'
Leads to happiness now,
Which is better than pie in the sky.

Chewing the Cud: Chapter Eight

- Go for the two birds in the bush.

- Sacrifice and suffering are natural and normal.

- Justice is organized fairness.

- Don't feel guilty if you're not.

- Forgiving does not mean forgetting.

- Missing a train is only painful if you run after it.

- Commitment leaves you free to be happy.

- Think less 'Why?' and more 'Wow!'

THE HAPPY ENDING

What are you doing here? This is the Happy Ending. Did you get here after reading the book or have you come straight here, hoping for a quick fix? If you are a quick fixer, you could be too focussed on the need for a happy ending. Perhaps you, more than anyone else, need to read the book! I'll see you back here later.

If you got here the hard way, congratulations! You made it to the beginning. That's right. You know there is no real Happy Ending – only a happy moment that is itself a new beginning. When the guy in the white hat rides off into the sunset, where does he go? What happens next? When Cinderella marries her Prince Charming, that's only the start of their life together.

Now is now, and it's good if it can be happy. But it is almost certainly not the end. So, the question is: where are you going from here? Happy risk taking!

References

Etymology

Throughout the book there are references to the origins or early meanings of words. These are mainly from the *Online Etymology Dictionary*, www.etymonline.com.

The Prologue

The book by Andrew Matthews is *Being Happy! A Handbook to Greater Confidence and Security,* Mediamasters (1988).

Chapter One: Being Different

The anecdote about the Society for Risk Analysis giving up on the definition of risk comes from Stan Kaplan (1997) 'The Words of Risk Analysis', *Risk Analysis*, 17(4), 407-417.

The quote about the iPod, 'We're making it less random to make it feel more random.' comes from Steven Levy (2006) *The Perfect Thing*, Simon & Schuster. Levy's book is *all* about the iPod and attributes the quote to Steve Jobs.

One popular definition of randomness says: 'the more complicated something is, the more random it appears'. This is known as Kolmogorov Complexity, after the Soviet mathematician Andrei Kolmogorov. Of course his

Complexity is a lot more complex than one sentence. Large expensive books have been written on the subject.

The anecdote about Democritus and the slaves meeting at the well is in the introduction to Juraj Hromkovič's book, *Design and Analysis of Randomized Algorithms*, Springer (2005).

Short people really do suffer health problems: Christensen, T.L. et al (2007) 'An evaluation of the relationship between adult height and health-related quality of life in the general UK population', *Clinical Endocrinology*, 67(3), 407-412.

Newton's obsession with the magic number seven is described by Patricia Fara in *Science: a four thousand year history*, Oxford University Press (2009). Fara says that, before Newton, artists mostly showed rainbows as having four colours.

For the theory that Newton and Einstein were Aspies see Ioan James (2003) 'Singular scientists', *Journal of the Royal Society of Medicine*, 96(1), 36-39. James says he consulted Simon Baron-Cohen, head of autism research at Cambridge University and they agreed it was 'fairly certain' that Newton and Einstein would meet the modern diagnostic criteria for Asperger's Syndrome.

We get more cautious as we get older, men seek more risks than women and tall people are greater risk-takers than short people. These claims are supported by many studies. All three are covered by Thomas Dohmen et al (2005) *Individual Risk Attitudes: New Evidence from a Large,*

Representative, Experimentally-Validated Survey, DP1730, IZA Bonn, available online at ftp.iza.org/dp1730.pdf.

When you are afraid, you are less inclined to take risks. When you are angry, you take more risks. See Jennifer Lerner & Dacher Keltner (2001) 'Fear, anger, and risk', *Journal of Personality and Social Psychology*, 81, 146-159.

The quote by Douglas Hubbard is from the preface to *The Failure of Risk Management*, John Wiley & Sons (2009).

Chapter Two: Happiness

Louis Armstrong may or may not have said, 'If you have to ask, you'll never know,' but it is certainly a popular anecdote. Eric Porter wrote a book called *What Is This Thing Called Jazz?*, University of California Press (2002). The title presumably refers to the popular anecdote.

At least 50% – possibly as much as 80% – of our potential for happiness is inherited. Alexander Weiss et al (2008) 'Happiness is a Personal(ity) Thing', *Psychological Science*, 19(3), 205-210. This reference also illustrates the use of the term 'set point' in connection with happiness.

Tall people feel happier than short people: Angus Deaton & Raksha Arora (2009) 'Life at the top: The benefits of height', *Economics & Human Biology*, 7(2), 133-136.

Daniel Gilbert's story comes from an interview he gave to Powells Books, posted online in March 2006, www.powells.com/blog/interviews/daniel-gilbert-stumbles-onto-something-big-by-dave.

Imagination plays a part in both thinking about the future and thinking about the past. There is a lot about this in Gilbert's book *Stumbling on Happiness*, Harper Perennial (2007). See also Daniel Schacter & Donna Addis (2007) 'The cognitive neuroscience of constructive memory: remembering the past and imagining the future', *Philosophical Transactions of the Royal Society*, 362, 773-786.

Robert Holden is director of The Happiness Project (www.happiness.co.uk) and author of *Happiness Now!* Mobius (1999).

In Uganda, 8% of children die before their first birthday; 31% of the population live in poverty. These figures, for 2009, are from the World Bank data sheet *Uganda at a Glance*: http://devdata.worldbank.org/AAG/uga_aag.pdf.

Lynne Friedli (2009) *Mental health, resilience and inequalities*, World Health Organization, uses a spectrum from 'flourishing' at one end to 'mental disorder' at the other. The report makes frequent reference to 'happiness'. www.euro.who.int/__data/assets/pdf_file/0012/100821/E92227.pdf

The text of *The Little Mermaid* by Hans Christian Andersen is available in many places online. For a beautifully illustrated recent publication that is true to the original story, see Christian Birmingham

(Illustrator) & Naomi Lewis (Translator) *The Little Mermaid (Illustrated Classics)*, Walker (2009).

The quote from Shakespeare's *King Richard II* is in Act II, Scene 1.

Darrin McMahon, *Happiness: A History*, Grove Press (2006), devotes over 20 pages in Chapter 6 to the American Declaration of Independence, and specifically the phrase, 'pursuit of happiness'.

The main Gareth Malone quote is from the soundtrack of the TV series made for the BBC by Twenty Twenty: *The Choir, Series 2, Boys Don't Sing*. The 'utter twit' quote is from an interview Malone gave to *The Observer*: www.guardian.co.uk/lifeandstyle/2009/sep/27/my-space-gareth-malone

The story of Edgar and Irma Rombauer is in Victor Geraci & Elizabeth Demers, Editors (2011) *Icons of American Cooking*, Greenwood. Irma Rombauer's book *The Joy of Cooking* was first published in 1931. The 75th anniversary edition was published by Scribner (2006). The expressions 'social intercourse' and 'gay musical gatherings' are from an article by Marion Rombauer Becker (Irma's daughter) on the *Notable American Unitarians* website: http://harvardsquarelibrary.org/unitarians/rombauer.html.

Alex Comfort's *The Joy of Sex* was first published in 1972. There have been many editions since.

CHAPTER THREE: WHY WORRY?

Expected shutdown dates for UK nuclear power stations are available on several websites, for example: www.world-nuclear.org/info/inf84.html. The figure of 3% for the contribution of Sizewell B is my calculation, based on published demand forecasts and the output of Sizewell B. In France, nuclear power accounts for nearly 80% of electricity demand: http://pris.iaea.org/public/CountryStatistics/Country Details.aspx?current=FR.

Nuclear power has a smaller carbon footprint than solar panels, according to the Parliamentary Office of Science and Technology, *Carbon Footprint of Electricity Generation*, Postnote No.268, October 2006, available online: www.parliament.uk/documents/upload/postpn268.pdf.

In the aftermath of the Fukushima nuclear accident, the German government announced on 30 May 2011 the closure of the country's nuclear industry by 2022: www.bbc.co.uk/news/world-europe-13592208.

The report from the Mental Health Foundation is Ed Halliwell (2009) *In the Face of Fear*. It is available free on their website: www.mentalhealth.org.uk.

The remark about Prozac is based on this study (and the media storm that followed its publication): Irving Kirsch et al (2008) 'Initial Severity and Antidepressant Benefits: A Meta-Analysis of Data Submitted to the Food and Drug Administration', *Public Library of Science Medicine*: www.plosmedicine.org/article/info:doi/10.1371/journ al.pmed.0050045.

Dollar Glen is owned by the National Trust for Scotland. One of the best descriptions, which includes the etymology, is David Beveridge (1888) *Between the Ochils and Forth*, William Blackwood and Sons: www.ebooksread.com/authors-eng/david-beveridge.shtml, Page 22 in this ebook version.

The idea that fear can increase the pain of childbirth has been around for decades, ever since Grantly Dick-Read (1954) *Childbirth without Fear*, Heinemann Medical Books. More recent evidence that a birth partner's fear during a caesarean can increase the mother's pain is in Edmund Keogh et al (2005) 'Psychosocial Influences on Women's Experience of Planned Elective Cesarean Section', *Psychosomatic Medicine*, 68, 167-174.

Daniel Kahneman was awarded the Nobel Prize for Economics in 2002: www.nobelprize.org/nobel_prizes/economics/laureates/2002/press.html.

The Reuters policy on the use of the word 'terrorist' is explained on their website: blogs.reuters.com/blog/archives/7146.

Kenneth Bogen & Edwin Jones (2006) 'Risks of Mortality and Morbidity from Worldwide Terrorism: 1968-2004', *Risk Analysis*, 26(1), 45-59. This study concludes that the lifetime chance of becoming a victim of terrorism (death or injury) is lower than 1 in 10,000. You would have to play the lottery a lot of times each year to get as good a chance of winning the jackpot.

The item about airport security in the British Medical Journal was Eleni Linos et al (2007) 'Did you pack your bags yourself?', *British Medical Journal*, 335,1290-1292.

CHAPTER FOUR: MAKING SENSE

Bees cannot see the colour we call red. Gumbert, A. et al (1999) 'Floral colour diversity in plant communities, bee colour space and a null model', *Proceedings of the Royal Society B (Biological Sciences)*, 266, 1711-1716.

The original experiments with upside-down glasses were done by George Stratton (1896) 'Some preliminary experiments on vision without inversion of the retinal image', *Third International Congress for Psychology*, Munich. Similar experiments have been done since. You can even buy inverting goggles online.

The blind can 'see' by listening to sounds through headphones. The website www.seeingwithsound.com includes a link to this research paper that shows the brain uses the visual cortex: Lotfi Merabet et al (2009) 'Functional recruitment of visual cortex for sound encoded object identification in the blind', *NeuroReport*, 20(2), 132-138.

The checkerboard illusion is available on Edward Adelson's website: http://web.mit.edu/persci/people/adelson/checkershadow_illusion.html. It includes further information, including proof that A and B are the same.

What is the risk of violence at the hands of the mentally ill? This is a good article available online: Oscar Hill

(2003) 'How much is violence associated with mental illness?', www.psychminded.co.uk/news/ news2003/may03/Royal College of Psychiatrists tackles issue of violence and mental health .htm. See also Tom Palmstierna (1999) 'Only about 1 in 30 predictions of assault by discharged psychiatric patients will be correct', *British Medical Journal*, 319, 1270, which shows that professionals as well as the public get this wrong.

People with mental illness are far more likely to be *victims* of violent crime: Linda Teplin et al (2005) 'Crime Victimization in Adults With Severe Mental Illness', *Archives of General Psychiatry*, 62(8), 911-921. Available online at www.archgenpsychiatry.com.

The study of doctors using different scales to assess mental patients is reported by Paul Slovic, et al (2000) 'Violence risk assessment and risk communication: The effects of using actual cases, providing instruction, and employing probability versus frequency formats', *Law and Human Behavior*, 24, 271-296. The study is also described in Slovic's book *The Perception of Risk*, Earthscan (2000).

The website quoted in connection with election fundraising is the Center for Responsive Politics, www.opensecrets.org.

Steven Levitt's research on campaign spending is described in Steven Levitt & Stephen Dubner (2006) *Freakonomics: A Rogue Economist Explores the Hidden Side of Everything*, Penguin.

The Swiss study that found a link between dementia and living near power lines is Huss, A. et al (2009) 'Residence near power lines and mortality from neurodegenerative diseases: longitudinal study of the Swiss population', *American Journal of Epidemiology*, 169(2), 167-175.

One billion people in the world do not have enough to eat. One and a half billion people are overweight. These are round figures. Nobody knows the exact numbers. The one billion hungry is estimated by the Food and Agriculture Organization of the United Nations, *Economic and Social Development Report*, September 2010. The one and a half billion overweight is estimated by the World Health Organization, *Obesity and overweight*, Fact sheet No.311, March 2011. 'Overweight' is defined as having a body mass index of 25 or more.

Even good clean water can be lethal in large quantities: www.scientificamerican.com/article.cfm?id=strange-but-true-drinking-too-much-water-can-kill.

The golfers who lost their skill by describing it appear in Kristin Flegal & Michael Anderson (2008) 'Overthinking skilled motor performance: or why those who teach can't do', *Psychonomic Bulletin & Review*, 15(5), 927-932.

More examples like the golfers are given by Malcolm Gladwell in *Blink: the Power of Thinking without Thinking*, Penguin (2006).

Chapter Five: Sharing

I know of two good studies on the risks of hitchhiking:

(i) Graeme Chesters & David Smith (2001) 'The Neglected Art of Hitchhiking: Risk, Trust and Sustainability', *Sociological Research Online*, 6(3), www.socresonline.org.uk.

(ii) Alice Garner (2008) 'Risk and reward: the (lost?) art of hitchhiking', *International Conference on Tourism and Leisure*, Chiang Mai, Thailand, www.ictlconference.com.

The quote by Frank Furedi is in the preface to his book *Culture of Fear Revisited: risk-taking and the morality of low expectations*, Continuum (2006).

Ken Welsh's guides had various titles over the years. The first one was *Hitch-Hiker's Guide to Europe: How to See Europe by the Skin of Your Teeth*, Pan Books (1971).

The blogger 'lynneguist' is M. Lynne Murphy. Her blog is at www.blogger.com/profile/10171345732985610861.

The survey to find out the things people thought to be typically English was conducted by the beer company Wells Bombardier in 2010.

The source for Claude Shannon's juggling and other 'totally useless things' is a tribute written by fellow juggler, Arthur Lewbel: www2.bc.edu/~lewbel/Shannon.html. It even includes a movie of the juggling clowns!

The serious stuff on information theory is Claude Shannon (1948) 'A mathematical theory of communication', *Bell System Technical Journal,* vol. 27,

379-423 and 623-656. It is available online: cm.bell-labs.com/cm/ms/what/shannonday/paper.html.

The MMR vaccine fraud was exposed largely by the work of the journalist Brian Deer, through his reports in the *Sunday Times* and his television documentaries. The whole story can be found on his website, briandeer.com.

The Duke University brain-scan study of younger and older women is Peggy St. Jacques et al (2008) 'Effect of aging on functional connectivity of the amygdala during negative evaluation: A network analysis of fMRI data', *Neurobiology of Aging*, 31(2), 315-327.

The quote by Peter Gabriel is from *Nelson Mandela and Desmond Tutu announce The Elders*, The Elders first press release, 18 July 2007, theelders.org.

The story of King Rehoboam in *The Bible* includes the verse, 'He disregarded the advice that the older men gave him, and consulted with the young men who had grown up with him and now attended him', 1 Kings 12:8.

For gender difference in the effect of mood on risk taking, see Helga Fehr et al (2007) *Risk and Rationality: The Effect of Incidental Mood on Probability Weighting*, University of Zurich Socioeconomic Institute, Working Paper No. 0703, www.sts.uzh.ch/research/workingpapers/wp0703.pdf.

The story about Newton and his 2060 prediction comes from Stephen Snobelen's website, *Isaac Newton: Theology, Prophecy, Science and Religion*, www.isaac-newton.org.

Newton wrote far more on religion and biblical interpretation than on the natural sciences and mathematics. His theological writings have been made available online by The Newton Project, www.newtonproject.sussex.ac.uk. The work, led by Rob Iliffe, was funded by the Arts and Humanities Research Council, www.ahrc.ac.uk.

CHAPTER SIX: TRUSTING

Research linking oxytocin and trust: Kosfeld, M. et al (2005) 'Oxytocin increases trust in humans', *Nature*, 435(7042), 673-676. Text available at www.zora.unizh.ch.

Robert Peston's blog about Northern Rock can be found at www.bbc.co.uk/blogs/thereporters/robertpeston/ 2007/09/rock_or_crock.html.

The quote by Stephen Green appeared in *The Independent* on 2 March 2009 in an article by Russell Lynch.

The quote by James Schiro comes from the article, 'Is it too risky to run a company?', *Managing Risk*, European Business Forum, Spring 2003.

This is the German study that found children's attitudes to risk and trust were similar to those of their parents: Thomas Dohmen et al (2006) *The Intergenerational Transmission of Risk and Trust Attitudes*, DP2380, IZA Bonn, available online at ftp.iza.org/dp2380.pdf.

There are many accounts of the first powered flights by Wilbur and Orville Wright. My best source was

Huffman Prairie Flying Field, American Institute of Aeronautics and Astronautics, *Historic Aerospace Sites* series (2002). Their website is www.aiaa.org.

One of the classic books on risk is Peter Bernstein (1996) *Against the Gods: The Remarkable Story of Risk*, John Wiley.

The quote by Peter Bernstein, suggesting that he changed his view over the years, is from a lecture he gave to the Chartered Financial Analysts Institute, 'Risk: The Hottest Four-Letter Word in Financial Markets', *Defining, Measuring, and Managing Uncertainty: The CFA Institute Risk Symposium*, New York City, 22-23 February 2006.

The Rembrandt painting: *Storm on the Sea of Galilee* depicts an incident described in the *Gospel of Mark* 4:35-41. The painting itself was last seen hanging in the Isabella Stewart Gardner Museum in Boston, Massachusetts. It was stolen in 1990 and has not been recovered.

The word 'faith' was not originally a religious word. The evolution of the meaning of 'faith' is described in the *Online Etymology Dictionary*, www.etymonline.com, under the entry for 'belief'.

The research that found trust to be low in poor countries and high in rich countries is by Paul Zak & Ahlam Fakhar (2006) 'Neuroactive hormones and interpersonal trust: international evidence', *Economics and Human Biology*, 4(3), 412-429.

There are many published accounts of the humanitarian effects of Operation Gatekeeper. One such is Maria Jimenez (2009) *Humanitarian Crisis:*

Migrant Deaths at the US-Mexico Border, American Civil Liberties Union, www.aclu.org/pdfs/immigrants/humanitariancrisisreport.pdf.

Likewise, there are many words written about migration to Europe. One serious, balanced account is Hein de Haas (2008) 'The Myth of Invasion: the inconvenient realities of African migration to Europe', *Third World Quarterly*, 29(7), 1305-1322. The text is available online at heindehaas.com.

The link between hopelessness and risk taking was studied in John Bolland (2003) 'Hopelessness and risk behaviour among adolescents living in high-poverty inner-city neighbourhoods', *Journal of Adolescence*, 26, 145-158.

Chapter Seven: Growing

The material on Bill Shannon comes from his website, www.whatiswhat.com, and from a feature article by Bill O'Driscoll, 'Turning the Tables: Artist and performer Bill Shannon keeps audiences off balance', *Pittsburgh City Paper*, 29 March 2007, www.pittsburghcitypaper.ws/pittsburgh/turning-the-tables/Content?oid=1335045.

Dick Fosbury's story is from an article by Kerry Eggers, 'From "Flop" to smashing high jump success', *The Portland Tribune*, 23 July 2008 (updated 30 October 2009), www.portlandtribune.com/sports/story.php?story_id=121684873519440400.

The material about heights of American and Dutch adults comes mainly from an article by Burkhard Bilger, 'A Reporter At Large: The Height Gap', *The New Yorker*, 5 April 2004, www.newyorker.com/archive/2004/04/05/040405fa_fact.

The idea of dealing with problem drinkers by addressing the alcohol intake of the general population has been around for decades.
It seems to have originated in Paris. Sully Ledermann (1956) 'Alcool, alcoolisme, alcoolisation: Données scientifiques de caractère physiologique, économique et social', *Institut National d'Etudes Démographiques*, Cahier 29, Presses Universitaires de France.
There is an online study guide in English at www.enotes.com, entitled *Prevention of Alcoholism: The Ledermann Model of Consumption*.

Romeo speaks the words 'Live and be prosperous' in Shakespeare's *Romeo and Juliet*, Act V, Scene 3.

The Legatum Prosperity Index™ is available online: www.prosperity.com.

CHAPTER EIGHT: LETTING GO

The 'Bird in Hand' pub mentioned at the start of the chapter has its own website, www.birdinhand.co.uk. I can't say whether it is haunted or not, only that it has been investigated by the Berkshire Paranormal Group.

Daniel Kahneman spoke about loss aversion and the ratio of 2:1 in his Nobel Prize lecture, *Maps of Bounded Rationality: a Perspective on Intuitive Judgment and Choice*,

8 December 2002, www.nobelprize.org/nobel_prizes/
economics/laureates/2002/kahnemann-lecture.pdf.
The 2:1 ratio is a widely accepted figure:
en.wikipedia.org/wiki/loss_aversion.

The goodbye kiss at New York's Newark Airport was
widely reported in the press. The closest to home I
could find is this report by Mike Frassinelli, writing in
the Newark-based newspaper *The Star-Ledger*:
www.nj.com/news/index.ssf/2010/01/newark_airpor
t_security_breach_1.html.

The distinction between pain and suffering was
pioneered by Eric Cassel (1982) 'The Nature of
Suffering and the Goals of Medicine', *New England
Journal of Medicine*, 306(11), 639-645. Cassel later
expanded this into a book with the same title,
published by Oxford University Press (1991).

The British 'fair play' quote is from *How fair is Britain?*,
Equality and Human Rights Commission, Triennial
Review 2010, Executive Summary,
www.equalityhumanrights.com/key-projects/
how-fair-is-britain.

The extract from the South African Interim Constitution
is available online in several places. One such is
www.justice.gov.za/trc/legal/justice.htm.

Desmond Tutu wrote about his experience on the Truth
and Reconciliation Commission in *No Future without
Forgiveness*, Random House (2000).

The South African study mentioned, which found a
link between forgiveness and improved mental health,

is Debra Kaminer et al (2001) 'The Truth and Reconciliation Commission in South Africa: relation to psychiatric status and forgiveness among survivors of human rights abuses', *The British Journal of Psychiatry*, 178, 373-377.

The book by Nassim Taleb about highly-improbable events is *The Black Swan: The Impact of the Highly Improbable*, Random House (2007) and Penguin (2008).

Havi Carel's story is in her book *Illness*, Acumen Publishing, Art of Living series (2008).

Timothy Chappell reflects on his climbing accident in an online publication: www.scribd.com/doc/3699294/ timothy-chappell-the-fear-of-death.

WHO IS STEVE MARTIN?

Steve Martin has an unusual personality. His mix of analytical ability and personal creativity enables him to structure complex material for easy understanding. He is also an accomplished public speaker. At the age of 14, he was performing as a magician, on stage and at children's parties. As an adult, he has experience over many years of acting and lecturing. He has recorded voice-overs and training material.

Steve worked for many years in the field of data collection for clinical trials, first with a cancer charity and then in the pharmaceutical industry. He established an excellent reputation both as a Project Manager and as a Communication Consultant.

Before that, Steve played many different roles in commercial and academic organizations: mathematician, software designer, electronics engineer and lecturer. His professional expertise in risk management is augmented by private study of the psychology and mathematics of risk over a period of 7 years.

Steve graduated from the University of Manchester in the UK, and later trained in Project Management and Teaching Methodology. He was a UK Chartered Engineer for many years. Steve has lived and worked in the UK, Singapore, Belgium and Switzerland. He and his wife are in the process of moving to Tanzania as volunteer workers. They have two sons, one in Australia and one in Singapore.

WWW.COOLRISK.COM

2117559R00123

Printed in Great Britain
by Amazon.co.uk, Ltd.,
Marston Gate.